little things
in the hands
of a big God

Also by Betty Pulkingham
with Jeanne Harper

SOUND OF LIVING WATERS
FRESH SOUNDS

little things
in the hands
of a big God

betty
pulkingham

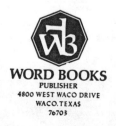

WORD BOOKS
PUBLISHER
4800 WEST WACO DRIVE
WACO, TEXAS
76703

LITTLE THINGS IN THE HANDS OF A BIG GOD

ISBN 0-8499-2855-9
Library of Congress Catalog Card Number: 79-63930
Printed in the United States of America

To my mother, Betty Carr, who taught me that when you have a steep and rocky road to climb it's best to take long, purposeful strides, walking slowly and steadily until you reach the top.

CONTENTS

The Seed — 9

1 A Long Way to Go — 15
2 Smoke Screen — 22
3 Going, Going, Gone — 29
4 A New Policy — 36
5 Carrots to Chew — 42
6 Hung up at Christmas? — 48
7 Mushrooms Live in Kings' Palaces — 53
8 Babies are Free — 59
9 The House on North Main Street — 66
10 Unstuck — 71
11 The Way In — 74
12 Divine Décor — 79
13 Where Thieves Break Through — 85
14 Culture Shock — 91
15 Diary of a Pilgrim — Part 1 — 98
16 Diary of a Pilgrim — Part 2 — 102
17 Not a Sparrow Falls — 107
18 A Steeple Chase — 113
19 A Tale of Two Trousers — 122
20 Wee Georgie — 127
21 Gale Warning — 131
22 A College Goes to Heaven — 138

A Short History of the Fisherfolk Ministries — 143

The Seed

To begin is the hardest part. To make a beginning. To point one's will in new directions and see by faith a completion. That's the hardest part.

This book begins on a busy street in Houston, Texas, in the spring of 1970. Perched high in the driver's seat of our family's Dodge van, driving east on Harrisburg Avenue towards Sears, the idea struck me. I should say the picture came to me, for it was not in fact an idea, but a picture of a book cover similar to the one you saw when you picked up this book. Why I have waited until now to begin the writing I cannot say with assurance, but seeds do have to be watered and nourished ere they sprout.

Many of the incidents described here reach back into the life of our parish family at Church of the Redeemer (Episcopal) between 1964 and 1972.

Beginning with a coming together of five families all experiencing a dramatic sense of calling to BE THE CHURCH, the fellowship gradually extended to include many others. The initial gathering was invited, although not in an official or institutional sense, by my husband, Graham Pulkingham, rector of the church, whose despair at the impotence of his own ministry led him to look for an honest redefinition of the ministry of Christ. Into what became a new organic ministry following sound Biblical principles came four laymen who were willing to leave everything else behind if need be in order, together, to exercise the ministry of Christ in that place and at that time. It was a compelling vision, and had dramatic consequences in their lives. Some left comfortable homes, moving into the changing neighborhood around the church. Some left high-salaried jobs and took less profitable ones close at hand. All entered into a new experience of being available to minister, whether that meant spending their time, their money, or opening their homes to one another.

The church became noted for the vitality of its worship life, its concern for the healing of souls, its theological emphasis on mature sonship in Christ, and its evolution of an extended-family lifestyle to accomplish the foregoing. The early years (1964–1968) saw the beginning of this alternative lifestyle and a heavy emphasis on Biblical teaching and pastoral care. There was no program of evangelism or outreach as such, but a growing number of people came to the church: some in search of healing (there were many kinds), many in search of a place of usefulness and training in the Body of Christ. Three such persons became members of the rectory household, involved along with me in supporting Graham's innovative leadership of a changing, growing congregation. These three were Bill Farra, a young widower still recovering from the death of

his wife; Arabella Miner, a recent university gradu-
ate; and my sister Nancy Carr, a teacher. Our roles
changed as needs in the congregation presented
themselves. On one afternoon I might be found
teaching a piano class to children (whose parents
had left behind such luxuries as private music teach-
ers when they moved into the inner city to be a part
of the Redeemer Ministry) while Arabella stayed
home and looked after the children. On another day
Arabella might lead Bible sharing at the church
while I did the week's laundry. Bill served the church
as organist and I as choir director; he also assisted
Graham in many parochial tasks. At home he was
an excellent handyman! Nancy supported us all—
quite literally—through her income from teaching
music in the Deer Park schools. But whatever any
of us were doing, there was the exciting sense that
every day was lived beyond ourselves—serving God's
called-together family in that place.

Many who came to the church out of their own
need to be ministered to remained to minister. One
such person was Nancy McCracken (called
Cracken), who became a part of the rectory family
in 1967. As people received healing and stayed to
pour out their lives in service to others, a pattern
of growth was established which would soon push
many from their spiritual nest to wing their flight
to many other parts of the globe. The opening of
The Way In coffeehouse on July 4, 1969 signalled a
new period of outreach, first into the city of
Houston, later through a travelling team ministry
into other parts of the U.S.A., and eventually into

11

England in September 1972. The renewed life of Redeemer Church began to kindle sparks of renewal in dozens of other churches of various denominations.

Today that life is being lived out around the world, as married people, single people, young and old, come together in Fisherfolk communities, laying at one another's feet their choicest treasures: their time, their leisure, their possessions, their plans for the future, their talents and abilities, because they have caught a vision of serving the church with the whole of their lives.

For our particular household, many changes were in store as we sought to follow the Lord in this new way of living. From the rectory next door to the Church of the Redeemer, where we lived as a family of twelve (Graham, our six children,* Arabella, Bill, the two Nancys, and me) we moved across town in 1968 to an urban area where, with an enlarged household of twenty, we set about developing the youth ministry which resulted ten months later in The Way In coffeehouse. This accomplished, others assumed oversight of the ministry and our own household relocated in a neighborhood near the church again. The rectory was now being used for other purposes, so we looked for the nearest house

---

* The youngest, David, was born in 1968. The other children were Martha Louise, age 3; Elizabeth Jane, age 6; Nathan Carr, age 9; Mary Graham, age 13; and William Graham (Bill), age 15.

we could find that would accommodate a dozen and a half people.

Shortly after we had settled into the spacious six-bedroom house on North MacGregor Way, I was chatting with a neighbor one day. She asked me, "Just how do you all sleep? Do you have sleeping bags for everybody?" I smiled. My grandmother's house was of comparable size and housed about as many people (all of whom slept in beds!) and no one thought it strange. How then, I wondered, has our definition of "family" and "normal" become so fossilized, so bound to the nuclear unit?

One thing I know: that I live in a family, and God has gathered us together from many places and persuasions to love one another and give ourselves to serve his church in a variety of ways. Our family here in Scotland includes five national and many denominational backgrounds, and we serve the church in a particular way through the development of worship resources (music, drama, dance) and through a travelling ministry which has extended to New Zealand, Australia, Sweden, Spain, and Germany.

"The mustard seed," said Jesus, "is the smallest of all seeds." Yet it grows into an enormous tree. And so it is with our lives. Each tiny part can be a seedbed where faith brings God's word alive. Our small things become his big things, our tiny offerings his kingdom's treasure, our widow's mites his riches in glory. Had anyone said to me twelve years ago that the little beginnings in Houston would spawn a work of the Spirit of God with worldwide

13

dimensions, I would have staggered with unbelief. As a matter of fact, someone did say it, did believe it—my husband, and I did stagger.

If you can forgive the staggering, the shrinking behind the wine-press, perhaps you will enjoy this book. I am one who, like Gideon, scarcely recognized himself when the Lord addressed him as a "mighty man of valour." Certainly I did not feel *fit for the battle, for tipping out the box in which my life was stored and allowing God to put it together in a different way. Yet here I am, twelve years later, with a story to tell. They are many stories really, and many people have a part in them. If I staggered at the big things, God in his mercy met me in the little ones.*

I offer you these little things from my life and the lives of those about me. With joy and reverence, with candour and simplicity, I offer them, to him and to you.

BETTY PULKINGHAM

January 1977

I

A Long Way to Go

"Come, look!" Graham motioned with a nod of his head towards the open window. I looked outside. We laughed. Our family car which we had driven all the way from Texas (arriving last night for a vacation at my parents' North Carolina home) was sitting by the kerb with two flat tyres.

"Looks as if we barely made it," I said. "How mightily our Valiant has fallen!"

"Looks as if the Lord was with us," responded Graham.

There he goes with the Lord again. The Lord this and the Lord that. Sometimes I think I'll scream.

"Yes, I'm sure he was," I said.

The unpacking of the car remained to be done. I sat down with a cup of coffee and a cigarette to fortify myself for the task.

What is the matter with him? He's so very holy all of a sudden. "Yes, that box of toys can just stay here in the den,

15

but could you take the suitcase into the bedroom? Thanks, Jim." *Better still, what's the matter with me, that I get so unnerved by his new religious zeal? I can remember a time when I was the family fanatic and he was the stoney intellectual. What has happened?*

*   *   *

The confusion of thought was typical of my state of mind in the summer of 1964. It had been a tumultuous year, beginning with our move to Houston in September 1963. I could still remember our first visit to the rectory. The retiring rector and his wife were the sole occupants of the comfortable two-storey home next door to the church. I was viewing the house through the eyes of a mother of four.

"And here," said the rector's wife, opening a door in the downstairs hallway, "is a handy cupboard for storing Christmas decorations."

Christmas decorations! I'll put them in the attic if you don't mind and use this for everyday things like the vacuum cleaner and baby stroller. "Yes, that's very nice," I said.

We ventured upstairs. I was intrigued by the location of both toilets, one just above the other, in full view of the front door. Should the bathroom door just happen to be ajar . . .

"Now here," Mrs. H. said with a sweeping gesture towards the cupboard-sized area adjoining the master bedroom, "is the nursery."

Well, I'm sure we'll put it to some good use, but don't count on that one. "Yes, that's lovely," I said.

"I know you will like it here very much," she continued as we returned downstairs! "No one ever bothers you."

My heart sank. *Oh dear, that must mean the parishioners have learnt to stay away. It sounds very lonely.*

"Yes, I'm sure I shall," I smiled back at her.

After we had taken our leave of the rector and his wife, we drove around Houston's East End.

"Where do the children play, I wonder." My eyes scanned the high metal fence around the schoolyard. The gates were padlocked. Coming from Austin's affluent suburbs, I was accustomed to spacious lawns and parks. There was nothing of the kind here.

"It's a far cry from Tarrytown, isn't it?" Graham read my mind.

"Indeed."

The move from Austin to the shifting sands of Houston's East End was difficult in the extreme. Only the Bishop's strong entreaty and Graham's equally strong desire to go to an inner-city church served to get me on my feet and moving. I thought frequently of Abraham and Isaac during those days. It seemed that God was requiring an awesome surrender of my children's lives into his hands. Ten-year-old Bill wept every morning before he left for school. The hurly-burly of the large city school was radically different from the encouraging intimacy of the parochial school he had attended in Austin.

There were problems of adjustment for me as well. The church women's guild system was decaying: there was one guild for the socially elite over forty; one for the homemakers over fifty; one for working women of all ages; and one for young mothers. I didn't fit anywhere perfectly.

Nor was I sure what to do with my musical training and gifts. Always before I had found a ready outlet in the place where we lived, and frequently as a complementary part of

Graham's ministry. When he was chaplain to a university medical school, I had organised a medical students' choir. When we were in a small mission church, I played the organ and directed a choir of volunteers. At St. David's, Austin, I had basked in the standards of excellence which this choir set in the city. But here? The choir director's strategy failed to command my respect. Relying on the operatic fervour of four hired soloists to cover the wavering sound of his past-its-prime soprano section, he made musical hash of many anthems by arbitrarily switching parts. ("Oh, there are no altos tonight? Well, never mind. Horace, will you sing the alto an octave lower?") I dreaded choir rehearsal night; it was an endurance test every time.

Then there was eleven-month-old Jane. Each night she would wake from a sound sleep not once, but two or three times, crying and shaking with fright as under her window an ambulance or fire truck screamed by. At first I thought she would adapt to the noise given a little time, but after a month I began to wonder.

There were other traumas that went far beyond our family and church life. One day in November I was shopping in a nearby supermarket. The usual canned music was missing and in its place was a radio programme: a kind of 'you are there' report of some historical event. Methodically, I walked from aisle to aisle collecting the humdrums of our weekly needs. There was little here to stimulate the culinary imagination; the store catered for the surrounding Mexican-American and black-American neighbourhoods and there was a meagre variety of goods available.

"Yes, it has been confirmed that the President has been shot," the commentator's voice came over the radio. It was obviously a play about a presidential assassination.

The voice on the radio droned on as I ticked off the items on my list. Just three more things to find.

... "And the police escort is leading the presidential car down the expressway towards Parkland Memorial Hospital."

Something stirred in my conscious mind. *Isn't that in Dallas?*

Baked beans. Tomato sauce. The big size.

... "The secret servicemen are escorting Mrs. Kennedy into the hospital now."

Suddenly the wheels of my grocery trolley ground to a halt mid-aisle and my body stiffened. My mind reeled under the staggering impact of what I was hearing. They were not talking about McKinley or Lincoln. They were talking about John Kennedy. They were talking about the man who only twenty-four hours ago had been escorted down the Gulf Freeway and given a real Texas welcome just two blocks from where I now stood. A wave of nausea swept over me and hot tears stung my eyes. I glanced around. Shoppers were shopping, the tin-ring of cash registers continued, the world around me plodded on in its mechanical quest for survival. Leaving the partially filled trolley in the middle of the aisle, I walked out of the store dazed, and fled home.

*   *   *

After such a tumultuous year, I was thankful for a time away, a real vacation at last.

"And so," Graham was saying, "I think the Lord is telling me I should go to New York."

We had been in North Carolina for less than a week. This was turning into a peculiar sort of family holiday.

19

"Did he obligingly tell you when you should go?" I said with icy sarcasm.

"Yes, he did. Next Tuesday."

I was speechless. But not for long.

"What do you intend to use for money?" It had taken some fancy figuring just to get us here. I couldn't imagine . . .

"I'm sure the Lord will provide and I do have a charge card for gas, in case you're worried," he smiled.

He seemed so untouchable in his logic, so unruffled in his responses, so unswerving in his resolve to hear God and do what he said. In my heart of hearts I admired him. In my flesh of flesh I was terrified.

Tuesday indeed. I suppose God has nothing better to do than to spin a wheel and tell us when to stop and when to go and what colour geraniums to plant.

But in my heart I knew he was on a quest that was real and earnest and that I wanted to go too, if I could just find out how. Actually, my God was not dead; he was just locked up in a cupboard somewhere, a closet filled with prayer books and hymnals and commentaries. My girlhood romance with him, my young adult zeal for good preaching and sound doctrine, both had faded under the grey reality of making it work. Making the church work. Making our family work. Neither felt like a viable Christian society to me, yet since my teen years I had known that there was somewhere, sometime, a powerful being-togetherness at the very heart of God's life.

It's not fair. I finally burst into the cupboard where I had God stored. *It's not fair that you tell him all these special secrets and when to come and when to go, and which Bible verses to read. You never do that for me.*

20

What's so special about him? I reckon you just do these sorts of things for ministers, is that it? What about the children and me? Do we just live off crumbs?

I really let God have it, I did. And a curious thing happened. That evening (it was Thursday, two days after Graham had left on his journey to New York) I had a very strong impression.

Ephesians 3: 15. I seemed both to hear and to see it. I wasted no time in finding a Bible and consulting this verse.

"Of whom the whole family in heaven and earth is named."

My first response was indignant. *What kind of answer is that? It's not even a complete sentence.* But then I saw the words, THE WHOLE FAMILY. They seemed to hop off the page right into my heart, assuring me that the Lord wanted to show himself not to Graham alone, but to all of us.

O thank you, thank you, thank you Lord. Forgive me. It doesn't matter to me whether you speak in whole sentences or not as long as you speak to me.

The breadth and length and depth and height of that little word 'family' was hidden from my view just then. But one thing I knew: God wanted all of us named Pulkingham to be swept up into his life of love in a new way.

And it began to happen.

2

smoke screen

The air was heavy with smoggy smells: the aroma of burnt coffee from a nearby factory mingled with exhaust fumes from trucks lumbering down Telephone Road. I sat in the dining-room and gazed out of the front window at who knows what. The meteorologists would have called it a sunny day (because they were not sitting where I was.) One thing about the hazy impurity of East End air, however: it lent itself to impressionistic meanderings as one sat and stared. All the edges of the world seem blurred, and not so sharp as they might have been. In that context it was easy to let one's mind wander down unaccustomed paths. On this particular day I had been reading a chapter in *The Cross and the Switchblade,* and suddenly it struck me: *Every day of my life I see youngsters like that wandering these streets.* I was recalling the young addicts described by David Wilkerson in his exciting book.

Every day of my life.

Some of them I knew by name, others not. And of course they were not on heroin — not yet. But it was only a matter of time. Many were sniffing glue, most came from frac-

22

tured families. All seemed to be reeling down the corridor of their jostling trainlife without balance or sense of direction.

O Lord, if you can do such wonders for young people in New York, you can do it in Houston too. Do it here. Reach out to these as well. Start a work like that in this place.

My soul's longing was deep and intense. New thoughts were born out of a strong yearning inside of me.

How can you be so sure that I can deliver them of their addiction when you will not let me deliver you of yours?

There it was. It was the same still small voice that had spoken to me for years but all too often had been hastily dismissed in the important busyness of my life. But there it was again, that gentle flower easily downtrodden, soft entreaty quickly drowned in decibels of ongoingness, that firm, clear, penetrating voice of truth.

One thing I grasped that I had never grasped before: the Lord for his kingdom's purposes was asking me to stop smoking. Always before my guilt about finances or self-concern over my own health had motivated me, without success. But now it came through to me, fresh and powerfully, that deliverance must be my experience before I could ask God to set others free.

And so it was that the battle for my soul began in earnest. (I didn't dream that's what it was then. Only in retrospect could I see it.) On the Lord's side were my children, who really disliked the smell of tobacco smoke.

"Mama, will you open the car windows? It's awfully stuffy back here," they would say. Or, "Mama, why do you like to smoke?"

And on the Lord's side also, to my surprise, was my husband who had smoked as heavily as I for years and suddenly stopped. Just like that.

On the opposing team was a host of accusing and discouraging thoughts.

If you stop, you'll get fat . . . you can't do it anyway. You've tried dozens of time, remember . . . It's really your parents' fault: if they had not prevented you from sucking your thumb as an infant you wouldn't have this oral need to satisfy . . . Come on, now, remember: you're a liberated Episcopalian, not a hardshell Baptist! Why don't you just cut down and smoke a few a day. After all, three cigarettes a day couldn't possibly hurt you.

These thoughts, sometimes threatening, sometimes condemning, sometimes sweetly reasonable, were my mind's accustomed furnishings. But a refurnishing job had begun, and the expertise of the interior decorator was showing through.

One day as I was waiting for my car to be serviced and strolling through an attractive salesroom of the service station, I found myself humming an old Gospel chorus. The tune was not one of my favourites and I barely knew the words but there it was, cheerily humming along in my head.

> Hallelujah, I have found him,
>   Whom my soul so long has craved.
> Jesus satisfies my longings . . .

As I walked past the sleek display case of the cigarette vending machine the words of the first verse came distinctly.

> Feeding on the husks around me
> 'till my strength was almost gone;
> Longed my soul for something better,
> Only still to hunger on.

One, two, three. I began to count half-aloud the brand names of the various cigarettes in the machine. Of the twelve available selections, I had tried, puffed, inhaled and purchased by the carton eight.

There is a sense in which I have quite literally been feeding on husks around me. It's really true. Why, even the number of brands I have tried is good evidence that these things offer no lasting satisfaction. I always seem to be looking for a better brand. Oh, Jesus, is it true that you really satisfy all our longings?

I felt the warmth and nearness of God's spirit assuring me that it was true.

Another day the interior decorator moved another piece of furniture in my mind. He said, *When you feel restless, you have a smoke. Why don't you talk to me instead?* It made me ponder. *Was this trail of smoke from my burning cigarette some sort of counterfeit incense?* Such simplistic thinking was not my accustomed way, but the impression remained with me.

Still another day I observed Graham settling down after dinner with a good book. He used to settle down for a smoke, but now it was always a chapter in some strengthening book.

Lord, you know how tempting it is to want to smoke after meals. I can't possibly stop what I'm doing and go read a book. There are the dishes, and the baby to change, and . . .

My thoughts to him trailed off in an endless round of duties. But he had heard my cry. The following day as I was doing the dishes a lightning-bolt idea struck me.

"All power in heaven and earth is given unto me."

I had learned the verse as a child. How could I have missed the impact of it? How could I have failed to see the Lord's great desire to use all that power on my behalf, simply for the asking? Surely ALL of that power applied to my smoking problem could avail something.

O Lord, I believe you have this power and authority over every form of evil. Lord, I believe it is available to me. Lord, by your help, I WILL stop smoking. I know I can. But, you know my weakness. I need some tangible reminder of your power, something to strengthen me right where I am, doing the dishes or whatever.

The very next day Graham and I attended a meeting on the west side of Houston; it was a noontime prayer group conducted by a new friend of ours who was a businessman. I was sitting with my head bowed praying with the others when I happened to glance at my hands. I gasped audibly: the tiny seed-warts (twenty or more) which had covered my fingers had completely vanished, leaving my hands clean and clear, without blemish.

Oh Lord God! What can I say?

My heart seemed to stand still.

You who formed the earth, whose power causes mountains to move, you, Lord, have stooped to answer me. By healing these hands you have given me a visible reminder of your power, for my hands are always with me, in the dishpan or wherever I go. Thank you, Lord Jesus.

And so it was that the Lord and I made contact. It would be nice to end the story just there, with the recounting of this miracle. For it was a miraculous event, and even more to be wondered at when Graham told his part. The night before he had awakened from a sound sleep, feeling moved to pray for me while gently laying his hand on my head. (The laying on of hands was a practice about which he had been seriously questioning the Lord.) In his marvellous economy, God had answered both Graham's prayer and mine.

The fact remains, however, that there was still an enemy lurking in my soul and one of sufficient strength to mar my freedom. I had cut down to one cigarette a day and it seemed impossible that there could be any harm in that — somehow. (This thought was the enemy.)

One day after finishing a smoke in the upstairs bathroom, being careful to blow the smoke out of the window to avoid telltale smells, I came down to the kitchen. This had been the second of three possible puffing periods — on the same cigarette.

Did you enjoy that? the Lord suddenly asked me.

Well, if I were to be perfectly honest, no, I didn't enjoy it very much, I answered him.

Neither did I, came his reply.

Somehow that surprised me, his putting it so straight and so simply. But then he said, *Well then,* his voice seemed relaxed and calm, *if you were not really free to enjoy it, and if I didn't take any pleasure in it, I wonder who did?*

This I pondered for a very long time. But of course. Who else? If I couldn't enjoy it and the Lord didn't enjoy it, the only one who could possibly be enjoying it was the devil himself.

The devil! How dare he? That old imposter! My soul's

greatest enemy. I refuse to give him another moment of satisfaction. Why the very idea! Lord Jesus, thank you for revealing his tactics to me. Why, the very idea!

The last useless piece of furniture had been moved. And I never smoked again.

3

Going, going, gone

November 1963. The alarm went off and I groped in the semi-darkness. I lay quite still, moving only my left arm to find the clock. Years of conditioning had taught me to take my time getting up. The terrible stiffness in my lower back was worse upon awakening and it was necessary to move very slowly with as little twisting or bending of the spine as possible. If I could just roll carefully from my back to my left side (which put me near the edge of the bed), then negotiate a rather intricate descent of my feet as I propped my body up on my left elbow, I could usually manage an upright sitting position. Frequently I would sit there for a few minutes readjusting to the new position and summoning the courage to stand. Standing was painful, walking offered some relief, lifting anything heavier than five pounds of sugar was ill-advised, and driving a car was excruciating.

*　　　*　　　*

"Eighty years old indeed," I murmured to myself on this particular morning. "Days like today I can believe it. Thank goodness Bessy comes to clean the house today!" Recalling our recent visit to John Sealey Hospital in Galveston and our consultation with one of its leading orthopaedic surgeons, I was pondering his diagnosis: a degenerative disc second from the last in my lower spine. This meant in practical terms, he had said, that the disc was four-fifths gone, and my spine resembled that of an eighty-year-old woman.

Today would mark my second visit to a physiotherapist whom he had recommended. A course of exercises and the full-time use of a back brace should relieve the situation somewhat. I was grateful to find the relief after years of attempted cures, including weeks of total bed rest in hospital and other periods of osteopathic treatment. Finally, we seemed to be getting somewhere.

And getting somewhere we were. I marvelled at the probing depths of the surgeon's enquiries into my past. From hitherto unexplored recesses of memory came several illuminating thoughts: first a picture of myself riding at a girls' camp when I was twelve, and then a puzzling afterthought. *Why did I ride with my teeth clenched?* Oh, yes, now I knew. As I recalled the cantering hoofbeats, I could feel a shooting pain with every canter.

"That's it!" I told Dr. Ainsworth. "I guess I was so determined to ride that I just put up with the pain, but it was definitely there when I was twelve." I smiled as I remembered how many times our children had called 'mommie' after being tucked in their beds with the lights out, and had shown me a cut or bruise hitherto unnoticed. I used to marvel how everything hurt only after it was put to bed. Then, I realised that the children were much too dedicated to their world of playing to be immobilised by minor pains. Only in the stillness of the night when activities had ceased did many of these 'so light afflictions' come to the surface.

"I want you to remember back before you were twelve," Dr. Ainsworth had persisted. "We still haven't hit upon the trauma itself."

My next impression was one of a rapid series of somersaults. As the incident came into focus, I could see in my mind's eye the hotel where I went twice weekly for piano lessons beginning at age eight. My lessons were in the ballroom and my teacher, a tall young college professor whom I adored, always walked with me to the head of the long marble staircase as I left. This day, as we were saying goodbye, I had tripped at the top of the stairs and hurtled downwards turning three hard-hitting somersaults before landing on the mezzanine below. I could still recall my teacher's chalkwhite face as he rushed down the stairs three at a time to my rescue.

Dr. Ainsworth nodded. "That sort of fall could well have caused the injury to the disc," he said with assurance.

*   *   *

November 1964. The alarm went off and I groped in the semi-darkness. A wave of nausea swept over me, very mild, but there it was, an oh-so-familiar feeling. To be pregnant again was not an easy thing. Hadn't the doctor said we definitely should not have more children if I wanted to find a way to live healthily with my injured spine? He had definitely said that. And I was definitely pregnant. There was no doubt in my mind. Out of this seeming

31

contradiction came a deep yearning — to prove God's good and acceptable will in this matter, to reconcile the irreconcilable. The past two months, more than any period in my life, had been ablaze with the radiance of the Lord's presence. It had been a time of learning to trust him in totally new ways, very conscious ways, committing my days and nights to him, and sensing his guidance in all the particulars of my life.

Why, he had even shown me how to throw away my 'list'. My list was the thing that told me what to do every day. I'm sure it began as a harmless aid to a busy homemaker, but it became a harness which prevented any flexibility, any freedom to do an unscheduled thing. Efficiency had become a prison with iron bars, and leisure a guilty business. The Lord in our new trusting relationship had said to me one day, *I want you to throw away your list.*

But why? I asked him.

Because there's no room on it for me to tell you a new thing. You've got it all figured out already.

Oh. And I knew exactly what he meant.

Since he had been admitted to the everydayness of my life, it was difficult to think that the Lord had overlooked something as basic as sex and babies. For here, too, I had put my trust in him. Could he have somehow fallen off his throne? I had tried 'the pill'; in fact, I had tried several varieties and each one had made me ill. Certainly I had heeded the doctor's counsel in other ways, the back brace and physiotherapy being cases in point; and I had attempted to heed it in this as well, but somehow nothing had worked. The Lord was definitely not helping me in my search for the right 'medical' solution. Did he have something else in mind? I had frequently pondered this; now I felt sure he must.

*　　　*　　　*

"Mother, are you going with us tonight?" Bill's voice sounded chirpily from the next room as he breezed through the doorway.

"Oh, that's right, it's already past six. When do we need to leave?"

"Daddy, when are we leaving?" he called back into the living-room.

"Just after seven," came the reply.

And so it was that we met outside the church — three carloads of us — just after seven, and drove to north Houston to a small Chinese-American Church to attend the Sunday evening service.

Thinking back, I could still remember eleven-year-old Bill's face on the first night he ever attended a service at Grace Chapel. It was during the 'battle' era when my soul seemed pushed and shoved in first one direction then another, seeking refuge and finding none. I was at once threatened and magnetised by the new life of obedience and servanthood which my husband espoused. Graham had told me about this curious little church where people greeted each other so warmly and encouraged each other in simple, direct ways ('Amen, brother'; 'Yes, amen'.) during times of teaching and testimony. And as he described the lively and peaceful quality of their worship, I was intrigued. Still, when Sunday rolled around I seemed to be doing other things and so it had happened that Bill, not I, went with his Daddy to the Sunday evening service. When they returned a new radiance shone from Bill's face, a glow which was unmistakable and real. From that moment I knew that I must go too. I must go and immerse my starchy churchself in the gentle dovelife of these people.

That had been months ago. And I had gone, not once but numerous times. Tonight was no different. We sang many non-Episcopal songs, some from a book, but all from the corporate heart of that congregation, songs that had become a part of them. As they sang, it was as if the people became a part of the songs as well, so tender and natural were the sounds they made; I experienced myself lifted out of the confines of my musical training into a new sensitivity to the spirit of God and what he wants to say through song.

During the testimony time, one of the men in the congregation told of a recurring vision he had had that day.

"Since early morning," Brother Wally said, "I have had a picture in my mind. It's a spinal cord, and the Lord keeps impressing me that it's brand new! I reckon that means healthy and whole. At any rate he just says to me that it's a brand new spine. And I just want to share that with you since it has been so much on my mind all day."

The service continued with sermon and songs. It took every ounce of my willpower not to jump from my seat and run to the front of the church shouting, "It's mine. I know it's mine. Don't you dare give it away before I get there. The Lord has heard my prayer and has fashioned a new spine for me. Hallelujah!"

But of course I didn't (still being an Episcopalian). My foot, however, was in the aisle at the end of the service. When a general invitation was issued for those who wanted prayer for particular needs, I bounded to the front of the

34

church where a small group gathered including Brother Wally.

There in the presence of God and that company I claimed the new back which he had offered me through his body. I claimed it, I thanked him, and we rejoiced.

*   *   *

The alarm went off and I groped in the semi-darkness. It was Monday morning following our Sunday visit to Grace Chapel. Without a moment's hesitation, I sprang to my feet.

"Praise God," I murmured as I stretched on my tip-toes and then bent from side to side. "My back is healed!" In the freshness of the morning dawned an awareness equally new. Startling. My back was as strong as anything, strong enough to do everything. Strong enough to lift a small child, to carry in the groceries, to bend and mop the floor.

And just to prove it the Lord took Bessie away (quite unexpectedly) to another job that Monday morning, leaving me the house to clean, the floors to mop. And I did it all.

4

A New Policy

The morning sun streamed in through the rectory windows as it had every other morning. But it had no warmth. The fast chill of frozen fears, too deep to be expressed in words, fell upon me as I groped for something to say. Nothing came out. The silence was strong.

I gazed at my husband. I saw a man who loved God and heard him say things clearly. I looked again. I saw a man who was dragging me over a precipice into a wild unknown, leaving behind all that felt secure. I looked a third time. I saw the father of our five children, and then it all came out.

"I can't believe God wants us to bring these children into the world and not make provision for their up-bringing," my words tumbled over each other, "in every way possible! It doesn't make sense to me. Who is supposed to educate them, then? Who but us? Why, the Bible even says that parents are to provide for their children and not the other way about." The longer I talked the more the words bounced from wall to wall, hollow-sounding.

"Well . . . ?"

Graham was silent. Then he said quietly, "I don't know what else to say to you. That's really all there is. I feel impressed that the Lord is asking me to lay aside all our life insurance policies and this endowment policy too."

He was referring to the twenty-year endowment policy for the education of our children. I could still remember the day we signed for it and the really good feelings I had had about it. After all, clergy incomes were not to be compared to most other professional salaries, and it seemed altogether prudent and a matter of parental discipline that we set aside this monthly sum out of our modest income to provide for the future of our children.

"Well, never mind about the life insurance. But what about the endowment policy? It's for the children, and they're the ones I'm concerned for . . ."

Or are you?

My thoughts struck home to the very core of my being.

Isn't it really yourself you're concerned for . . . frightened for? What if this noble experiment in communal living folds up on top of your heads . . . What if Graham dies . . . Then where will you be? Who will provide for you then? . . . or for the children?

Suddenly I realised how far I had yet to go along the pathway of trust, especially when it involved God in others, even those I counted as friends and brothers in Christ. It was not that I didn't want to trust them. I just didn't trust them in an ultimate and unconditional sense. Yet I could see in Graham a firm determination with which I had become well acquainted. He was convinced that as the shepherd of a flock who were committed to following the Lord all the way, he must lead the way in new areas of trust and commitment. I knew that.

Over the next two days I was like an insect whose wing has been caught in the fast closing of a window: trapped and helpless, pinned down but still struggling to be free. But there was no moving the window. And there was no changing Graham's mind. I began to search God's word for help and strength. And every time I opened my Bible a telling verse leapt out. One day I read "He who ministers the gospel must live by the gospel." And the next "Cast all your care upon him for he cares for you." Even the lilies of the field and fowls of the air were waving and winging their way into my conscious mind.

My mind said, 'yes'. *God knows what is best. God cares for me. He really does.* But there was resistance in my heart. I could feel it. What a place of frustration and torment: to know God is speaking, to give intellectual assent, but without one's heart's approval.

Two days later I had a very frank conversation with the Lord. *I know you are speaking to me in your word, Lord. And I know you have been faithful to provide what we need. You have shown me how you are perfectly able to care for us without my anxious worrying or fretting. Why, the times I used to use all my wits to try to balance our budget, it never seemed to work out peacefully at all, and I had a knot in my stomach every month that rolled around when the books had to be balanced again! Since then you have shown us so much: how to get free of our reliance on charge accounts, so we can spend what we have, instead of what we don't have yet. You took Graham to New York to see David Wilkerson and provided for him every step of the way. and I really can't say you have ever left us stranded, or hungry. What is this terrible fear about the future, then? Please send your Spirit to convince me, once again, in the ordinariness of my life, that you can manage our affairs better than I can.*

Having finally committed my will in the matter to the Lord, I felt much freer that day to go about my chores with a song in my heart. It was the day for weekly shopping at an East End supermarket. Off I went, with the usual shopping list and a quick look around the cupboards to see what staple items were running low. We were very short of cleaning supplies, I noticed. Scouring powder, furniture polish, floor wax, oven cleaner . . . the list went on and on. *Well, no wonder,* I thought, *these are pretty costly items, some of them anyhow. And we have been counting our pennies pretty closely these last few months.*

But somehow today was different. I entered Weingarten's with a sense of purpose and abandon. Not stopping a single time to deliberate about the items, I walked with easy precision from aisle to aisle, reaching high for the lemon-oil polish, stooping to scoop up a sack of sugar, collecting the little items quickly and easily from here and from there. I seemed almost to be gliding through the store, so smoothly did one motion follow another. No sooner had I placed something in the shopping trolley than my eyes would fall on something I needed across the aisle, and the wheels of the cart never stopped rolling until it was all accomplished. I stood at the check-out counter, took a deep breath and thought to myself, *Wow! That went smoothly. I didn't even stop to look at my list.* But (glancing over the list) I had remembered everything. Even a few things that weren't on the list. *Yes, I'm sure I have everything we need.*

The girl at the check-out counter was ringing up the items as I took them from the basket. *I surely bought lots of taxable items today,* I thought. *It's a good job I didn't try to keep a running total in my head the way I usually do. Too complicated with the tax and all.*

"That will be $8.57," said the girl behind the check-out counter.

I looked in my wallet and was slightly surprised to see only one $5 bill. *I thought I had more money than that,* I told myself. *That's really silly of me. I should have looked sooner and been more careful what I bought. There was really no need to get everything we needed today.*

There were two $1 bills in the wallet, but that still left a balance of $1.57. *There can't possibly be that much change. I shall have to take something back. Let's see, there's $8.25 . . . thirty-five . . . forty . . . forty-five . . .*

"I'm sorry about all these pennies," I told the check-out girl. "Actually, I'm afraid I'm a little short . . . there's fifty . . . fifty-one, fifty-two, fifty-three . . . no, that's a button, sorry . . . fifty-four . . . fifty-five." My thumb and forefinger pulled out a penny that was wedged in the corner of the billfold.

"Fifty-six," I announced tentatively.

"Oh, that's all right," the girl said pleasantly. "You can owe me the other penny."

I stared at her for a moment. My hand reached down into the deep recesses of the handbag I was carrying. "Yes, thank you, I appreciate that, but . . ." still groping in the corners, "somehow, I think it's here somewhere."

40

She looked at me quizzically, but waited patiently while I plumbed the depths of the handbag.

"There!" Up from the dark regions of tissues, key rings, note pads and gloves came a very grubby, ordinary and inconspicuous red cent.

"I just knew it was there," I said, and my face was tingling with excitement. She turned towards the cash register with the money, and my heart sang.

He knew it was there. The Lord knew it was there. Not only that. He knew everything we needed and helped me find it all. I never stopped to fume or fuss over what to leave behind. I bought every single item we needed, and I had exactly the amount of money needed — to the penny.

Making my way to the car with a sense of benediction, I pondered how marvellously the Holy Spirit had come in answer to my prayer: to convince me, once again, in the ordinariness of my life, *that you, Lord, can manage our affairs much better than I can.*

5

Carrots to Chew

The young dental student motioned to his professor and they drew close, beaming the adjustable light straight into my open mouth. The sucking noise of the metal piece in my mouth punctuated the silence, drawing saliva through a slender tube and away.

Dick, the senior dental student tapped my tooth and looked quizzically at the professor.

"It's like a fine, hard porcelain. I can't identify it. Can you?"

He stared intently into my mouth.

Then he shook his head slowly. "I don't recognise it."

While the two stood there, another professor entered and joined the gaping.

"Can you identify the material used in this filling?" Dick asked him.

He peered for a few moments, then shrugged and with a lift of his eyebrows answered, "No, I can't."

From my semi-horizontal position, I gurgled, "Which tooth is it?"

Dick obligingly held a mirror for me to see.

"Oh, that one!" I exclaimed.

My thoughts suddenly flashed back three years to a women's meeting at Redeemer Church. Our speaker that morning had been a middle-aged woman of sturdy build and great personal warmth. Her story held us spellbound. She told how she had entered a hospital in Reno, Nevada, in the final paralysing stages of multiple sclerosis. She told how she had taken along her bedroom slippers, believing that she would walk again, how the doctors had abandoned her life to the ravages of the disease, and how, later on, she had walked down the corridors of that very hospital, to the glory of Jesus Christ and the stunned amazement of the medical staff.

After the meeting we chatted with Gertrude Tyser about her life and ministry. It was clear that God's mighty miracle had been for her a springboard to a life given over entirely to his service.

"Won't you come and have lunch with us at the rectory?" I asked, really keen to have more time with her.

"I'd love to," she answered.

A few minutes later, as I stood staring into the refrigerator for the makings of a hasty lunch, I remembered how a friend of mine often prayed for the Lord's guidance when cooking. There was certainly not time for my usual careful planning, and the contents of the fridge did not look promising.

As I stood there letting the cool air out and the Lord in — to my pondering, a simple directive came to my mind.

Serve carrots. That's what he said.

"What a funny thing to start with," I murmured. But there it was. *Carrots.* I rummaged through the vegetable crisper and there were four carrots, just waiting to be discovered.

Scarcely enough to cook. I paused, then thought, *Of course! We can have carrot sticks.* Out came the lettuce as well as the carrots, and my thoughts were tumbling along with them. *And tuna salad, and these pickles. Hooray! Simple and nourishing.*

Lunch had seemed almost to put itself together that day. My thoughts were dancing back to the morning with Gertrude. What a radiant reminder she was of the authority of Christ over every form of evil, including the crippling disease she had suffered.

Then there was the dentist friend she mentioned, I pondered. My thoughts raced back to my dental appointment three months ago when a large filling had been put in my tooth, so large that it plunged away down into the gum line.

"You'll probably have trouble with this," the dentist had said. "It's so very large. Don't be surprised if you have to come back."

And trouble is exactly what I had. From the moment the novocaine wore off the pain was strong and intense. And in the very midst of it, before I could collect my wits to ring the dentist or to find the aspirin, a deep impression from within me let me know that the Lord wanted to heal this tooth himself.

The weeks that followed were difficult. The pain was always there, and many times it seemed unbearable. One night, when it was so intense I could think of nothing else, I stole into the nursery beside my bedroom and knelt to pray. No one was in the house save me; all, even the children, were next door at the church. In the unaccustomed stillness, the pain throbbed with every heartbeat, echoing throughout my nervous system. But something else was going on as well. In spite of the relentless pain, there was a great lucidity of thought. I knew that Jesus was Lord over this pain, I knew that his spirit lived in me, I knew that the pain was preventing my doing the work he had given me to do. So the spirit within me became indignant with this pain, and moved me to utter a bold strange thing.

"In the Name of Jesus, I command this pain to leave my body." The excruciating pain left and never returned. Something else left too. A deep dread of pain, a fearfulness to endure it, seemed to wash away as the waves rolled over my soul, leaving it somehow cleaner, clearer, like a sandy beach after a stormy tide.

Still, the tooth reacted with painful twinges when I chewed on it, and I had to chew on the other side of my mouth — carefully. Clearly the Lord's healing was not complete.

Arabella was bringing Gertrude in through the side door, and I hastened to greet them. When we had settled ourselves at the table around our simple lunch, we were entertained by our daughter Jane's rendition of the latest top-of-the-pre-school-pop tune. Fair-haired and delicate of stature, it was always a shock to hear this dainty four-year-old belt out nursery tunes and Sunday School choruses in a husky alto voice!

Plates were served and we passed the salad. Gertrude bit into a carrot stick quite audibly and exclaimed, "It's just wonderful to be able to chew carrots again! Ever since my dentist prayed for my tooth, I haven't had a bit of trouble!"

Carrots ... carrots ... carrots ... carrots ... carrots ... carrots ... of course, Lord! You knew she would say that. You knew she would tell me how you healed her teeth.

Somewhere deep inside me a key turned in a lock and opened yet another door on this adventure of faith. I had not gone this way before, and every trusting step was new, like those of a child who is holding on to his father's finger as he takes his first faltering steps.

When I asked Gertrude to pray for my tooth, she was quite surprised really, never having done such a thing before. Praying for teeth was certainly no speciality of hers (nor was it a custom of mine to ask dinner guests to pray for me!). She did so simply, asking that I be able to use the tooth normally, for chewing. And the Lord answered. From that time on I was able to chew. The Lord had healed the tooth — but more than that — he had taught me a priceless lesson in listening, in following the leading of his Spirit, of waiting expectantly to see him accomplish those things he had first of all whispered to my heart.

*   *   *

"Oh, that one!" I exclaimed. "That's the tooth the Lord healed — after much prayer."

The professors had gone on their way, and I was alone with the young dentist. He looked at me quizzically.

I was pulling my lower lip down so I could see the tooth better.

"Isn't that funny? It never occurred to me to look at it. Now I can see that it looks quite different from the filling that was originally put in."

"Well, it's definitely a substance which I can't identify," he said, gazing at me thoughtfully.

I smiled at him merrily. "It's definitely a tooth that

didn't work, but now does. I can tell you that. Funny how I never even bothered to look at it."

It's definitely your very own tooth, Lord. Thank you for another exciting chapter in the adventure of following you.

6

Hung up at Christmas?

"Graham, they won't understand."

"What won't they understand?"

"Why we're not sending any gifts this year. But more than that, that we're asking them not to. That seems so presumptuous — telling them what to do that way."

"Not exactly telling . . . asking, I believe. Well, at least it's an honest statement of where we are, and it will give them a chance to respond accordingly."

"Yes . . ." My eyes filled with tears as I thought about my own parents and how much it meant to them to send presents to the children at Christmas, especially since they lived so far away and could see the children rarely. It felt so depriving . . . not just to the children, but to them.

There was Graham's family too. Christmas gatherings and festivity seemed to be high on their scale of values. Of course, with more than twenty grandchildren, one needed a headache remedy to sort through the gift exchanges. Still . . .

I stopped to ponder what Christmas had been like these past years. I had a mental picture of myself wrapped in a tangled mass of package ribbons of all sorts and colours, struggling to get free. *Yes,* I thought, *it has been a cluttered season with never enough time or enough money to do all that seemed wanting.* When I started planning further ahead and organising myself better, the whole thing seemed to get even more complex, more fraught with tensions. Postal deadlines for foreign mail (Graham's relatives lived in Canada), school parties to be planned as a grade-parent, fitting the extra baking into an already packed schedule, making a list and checking it twice, or three times, lest someone should be forgotten, planning choir music for one of the Church's major festivals, scheduling extra rehearsals . . . On and on the thing grew.

I could remember several times in recent years sitting down to a gorgeous Christmas dinner and being too exhausted to eat. Small wonder then that around the first of December each year a tight knot developed in my stomach and never went away until after the bills were paid in January!

"The fact is," Graham was saying, "we are going to have to take a pretty radical step to get out of the trap we're in. I don't think we can make compromises."

"It seems radical enough to me if we write and tell our families that we are not sending them any gifts this year. But can't we leave them free to decide the rest — I mean about the kids and all?"

"That's the compromise I mean."

"But I don't think they would understand your idea that giving to the poor would be a substitute for exchanging gifts in the family."

"It's not just a matter of giving to the poor. It's a matter of helping our children out of the 'gimme' trap of

Christmas. And we need the help of our well-intended relatives to do it!"

I pondered this, and Graham continued, "I'm sure there are plenty of other opportunities during the year to send gifts to the children if they so desire. It's disassociating 'getting' with Christmas that I'm keen about."

"Yes . . . I can tell."

"And I'm not hung up on giving to the poor in some mechanical way either. I'm trusting the Lord to show us how we can meet the needs of whomever he shows us."

I was beginning to absorb this new way of looking at Christmas and certainly no one was more eager than I to simplify the whole operation . . . and if we could please God at the same time then so much the better . . . when suddenly I gave a start.

"The easy-bake oven!"

"The what?"

"Oh . . .! I don't think I ever told you, but several weeks ago Jane asked me if she could have an . . ." My voice began to trail off slightly, ". . . easy-bake oven for Christmas. It's one of those toy ovens that really bakes things." At the end my voice sounded apologetic.

"And you told her yes?"

"Well, not exactly. But you know how it is. I certainly didn't discourage her. And at this point, as far as I can tell, her heart is set on it."

Graham looked at me, and I looked at him. And in the exchange of glances I could tell this was another one of those compromises.

"It makes me feel so helpless," I pleaded, "when I've led her to expect it that way. She'll be terribly disappointed."

"We need to do what the Lord has told us," Graham's voice was firm, "and trust him with all these details."

"Details!" I exploded. "When your child's ability to trust is at stake, it feels like more than a detail."

"I didn't say details aren't important. I said we need to obey, and let God work out the details."

I sighed with a sigh too deep for words.

* * *

Over the next few weeks we began to share within the household the new theme, the poverty of spirit, which the Lord was bringing to our attention this Christmas. The children responded remarkably well, considering that they were, after all, children. But I still had not found a way nor had the courage, as of the first of December, to talk to Jane about what seemed like 'our' problem. A five-year-old girl with blonde curly hair, dancing blue eyes and a fanciful imagination could be difficult to bring down to earth with a thud.

So it was with a mixture of amazement and bewilderment that I heard Jane tell me that morning, "Oh, mother guess what! I had a vision last night. And it was Jesus. I mean, I could see him and everything!" Her voice rang with authentic excitement. "And you know what he told me?"

"That's wonderful, honey. What did he tell you?"

"He said, 'Jane.' I could hear him speak my name. He said, *Jane, I'm going to send you an easy-bake oven.*"

A dumb silence.

I could hear Jane reiterating the whole story in her typical Sara Bernhardt fashion. She had always had a flair for the dramatic. But this . . .

51

"Yes. Well ... You know, honey, sometimes, when we want something very badly, I mean very, very badly, we can even imagine that we're going to get it."

"No, mother. You don't understand. It wasn't imagination. Jesus really did come and talk to me."

I looked into her young eyes, and all I could say was, "All right, honey, I believe you."

I was still pondering what all this meant, and the irony of it, when the children left for school and I began clearing up the dishes; and still later in the morning, when the doorbell rang and I answered to find Mr. Brown, our smiling postman.

"Package for you today. Sign here, please, ma'am," he said in his usual jaunty manner.

I took the package and thanked him. "Hmm, it's from the Smiths in Austin. We haven't heard from them in a long time." My eye fell on the address. "It's to Jane," I mused. Then I noticed the card which was taped to the outside of the package. Opening it I read "This is a belated birthday gift from your godparents. We wish you many happy hours with your easy-bake oven."

And I closed my eyes and stood for a moment, just holding the package and offering thanks to the God who really does look after details when we look after obeying, who knows his children and their needs so perfectly, who delights in giving us the desires of our hearts as we set our hearts to follow him.

Always.

7

Mushrooms live in Kings' Palaces

Sally had come to chat while her husband was next door at the church. A young Episcopal clergyman, eager for a first-hand look at the 'gathered' quality of our life at Redeemer Church, he had brought his wife and two young sons from a neighbouring state. They too were experiencing the fresh new blown-upon-ness of the Spirit's awakening power in their small-town parish. There was much they wanted to know, were eager to learn. We had been chatting over the cleaning up of the lunch dishes, but now they were done.

"Why don't we take our coffee and have it in the living-room?" I ventured.

We settled ourselves in the cheerful white walled, gold carpeted room and then I wondered if it was the best thing after all, because, now that we were away from the func-tionary familiarity of the kitchen, Sally seemed tense.

"The rectory certainly is pleasant enough." Sally's voice trailed off tentatively. One sensed a hidden agenda.

"Well, yes," I laughed, "it's cheerful now. You should have seen it when we first moved in! The house had been decorated in the forties and all the downstairs walls were dark greenish-brown — the most depressing colour I have ever lived with! But that wasn't the half of it. Once the vestry approved the repainting project, the fun had just begun. We chose white to lighten the house inside, and even after two heavy coats of paint, the dark stain continued to show through. I thought we would never get it covered."

I pondered.

"What I mean is — it was two years before it was really completely white! I think the Lord taught me a lot about patience through having to look at those walls every day."

"Do you mean patience with the painters? They certainly took a long time getting it done!" Sally said emphatically.

"Well, I do mean that. And the vestry too. They were responsible for many other pressing needs at the church, but sometimes I was tempted to say, 'Why did they ever start this painting job if they didn't intend to see it through?'

"But I mean something else as well. I think it has to do with wanting everything around you to be perfect . . . yes, that's what it is. The Lord used two years of white paint with greenish-brown showing through to convince me I could ignore imperfections and still be happy!"

I smiled at Sally, and she smiled back. I thought she was beginning to relax a bit.

Then she said, "Well now, tell me — you know, about the 'extra' people in your house. It just seems to work fine and all, but . . . just how do you feed them? I'm sure you don't have a larger income than you used to when you were buying groceries just for your family."

"That's right," I said. "As a matter of fact, we don't get

a set income at all. The money that used to be Graham's salary is combined with whatever gifts come in to support the church's ministry, and it all gets divided up amongst those who are serving as full-time ministers here. That's the principle of it anyway."

"How can that possibly work?" Sally asked simply.

"Only if the Lord makes it work. I really don't know how it works, in any detailed sense. But I do know that we are eating! So maybe we can talk about that, since it's specific. Let me tell you about the greengrocer."

"That sounds English."

"Yes, it is. Our good friend and parishioner Douglas Luther is a bit of an Anglophile. He lives on the west side of the city and he's the one who introduced us to the green-grocer.

"But the story goes back still further. About a year ago a missionary and his family visited the parish. They had been living on the west coast for a time, and described to me the wonderful way the Lord had led them to a certain supermarket, where they were able to go each day near closing time and get vegetables and fruit that were being tossed out."

"Tossed out?" Sally queried.

"Yes. They were full-ripe and good to eat but some had slight blemishes or bruises and were being discarded. The missionary explained how her family was able to enjoy many wonderful fruits and vegetables which they would not have been able to buy at retail prices.

"And the funny thing was that as she was telling me this it was as if the Lord was whispering in my other ear and saying, 'Remember this. Now you will see me do the same for you.'

"So I was scarcely surprised when Douglas rang up one day and asked if we would possibly be able to use some fruits and veggies from his greengrocer friend. According to him, the housewives in River Oaks won't touch a piece of fruit with a blemish (it's a very posh place) and so the produce must be culled through frequently. He and his roommate couldn't begin to use all that the greengrocer was giving them.

"Naturally I told him we would be interested! I almost said, 'We've been expecting your call!' "

"Be back in a minute." Sally excused herself to check on the baby who was napping upstairs.

Now I remember. The very first time Douglas rang he didn't tell us all of that. He was probably embarrassed to ask us if we wanted someone's 'hand-me-down' food, even though he ate it himself and knew it was good! Instead, he asked if Graham liked fresh mushrooms, and I said he loved them. And he asked if I would object if he drove over every week and brought him a basketful, and I said I wouldn't object at all!

And that was the feeler. It must have been the next week that he rang and unloaded the whole story.

"And so," (Sally was back now from changing the baby) "starting then we became the weekly recipients of unexpected fresh treats — all of them extremely nutritious. Sometimes there were enough apples to make apple sauce for a whole week, other times lettuce was the big thing, and we used it in salads, shredded it, wilted it and did everything except put it on our ice-cream!"

Sally seemed to have something on her mind, but it wasn't at the verbalising point so I carried on.

"I must admit that sometimes we had weird combinations. The funniest, I think, was the week of turnips and red cabbage." The remembrance of it made me laugh.

Sally looked blank. *Exactly the way I felt when I first laid eyes on the back of the pick-up truck laden with boxes upon boxes of tired turnips and onions, colourful red cabbage, and very old, yellow corn too tough for your horse to chew!*

"I couldn't imagine what to do with it all," I said to Sally. "Up until then the Lord had sent us a much more appealing assortment than this and I was inclined to think there had been some mistake in his plan.

"But Graham came out to the carport and looked at the situation from his experienced gourmet's-eye-view.

"'A relish,' he said. And there was a let-there-be-ness about it that reminded me of the time the Spirit brooded over the waters and God spoke and created those first impossible somethings out of nothing. For a relish was definitely something and what I saw before me on the pickup truck was as near nothing as I could imagine in vegetable form.

"Well, there was relish, I can tell you. We rounded up half a dozen faithful helpers in the church kitchen and began to pare and peel and chop — and before the day was over there were close to fifty quarts of a wonderful-tasting, scrumptuous plum-coloured relish thereafter known far and wide as 'G.P.' relish."

"Because Graham made up the recipe?" Sally asked.

"Yes, and because no one was about to call it what was in it! Best that it remain a mystery. I think that ever since I have had a deeper understanding of God's redemptive process."

Sally lifted her eyebrows questioningly.

57

"Because — if God can take that unlikely looking bunch of second-hand vegetables and make a beautiful and tasty relish, who can tell what he can do with the likes of us?"

Sally was going to say it now. The hidden agenda item that hadn't come to the surface before.

I could tell by the way she was inching forward in her chair, her brow slightly furrowed, and her thoughts obviously martialled in single file towards a goal as yet undisclosed.

"That's really nice, how the Lord has been providing for your household — and others too — that way. He has obviously stretched your food budget enormously.

"There's just one other thing I want to know. How shall I put it? I believe that your basic needs are being met; I can really see that now. And maybe that's all I should want to see.

"But let me just ask you." She was very close to the seat's edge now, her voice slightly hushed, as though she was about to share one of her best secrets.

"Does the Lord ever send you — well, you know, something special ... something really good? ... like — (she was obviously groping for a food that was the epitome of luxurious living) — like MUSHROOMS?'

"Mushrooms," I echoed, unable to conceal a smile. "Funny you should ask about them! Yes, as a matter of fact, he *does* send us mushrooms. Big basketsful."

Sally's eyes widened.

"Every week." *I'm so proud of you, Lord.*

8

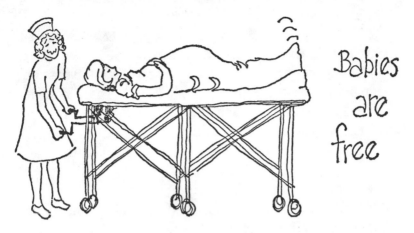

Babies are free

The smell of burning bacon filled the rectory kitchen and slowly invaded the rest of the house.

"Betty ... Betty, are you up there?" I could hear Arabella's voice calling up the attic stairs.

"Oh—yes, I'll be right down." I quickly stacked the blankets and diapers in a neat pile, closed the trunk and made my way past the boxes and oddments we had accumulated for storage.

There! I thought with satisfaction, *at least that's something. I couldn't bear to go to the hospital without unpacking the baby clothes.*

Sideways glances met me at the breakfast table. I hastened to explain:

"Oh—all of you, I'm really sorry about the bacon. I never should have gone to the attic while it was cooking."

"That's all right, Mom. We've had good practice, you know, scraping our toast every day," fifteen-year-old Bill gently teased. Everyone laughed.

59

"It's a little more difficult to scrape burned bacon," Graham commented wryly.

He was right. How stupid of me just to walk out and leave it. Whatever had possessed me . . .

"I know what you were doing," Arabella interrupted my searching thoughts with a twinkle in her eyes. "You were out gathering leaves and twigs."

"Leaves and twigs?" Bill queried.

"Yes. You know — like a mother bird when she builds her nest. It's something like that."

Our eyes met, agreed.

"Well, as a matter of fact, this morning when I first hopped out of bed, I had this very familiar feeling — like a mild contraction."

All eyes met mine.

"It's early."

"Yes, a month. Well, never mind. It's probably a false alarm, and maybe the Lord's way to get me unpacking the diapers."

My mind made a stronger case for the real thing: the actual beginning of labour.

*   *   *

This would be our sixth child. Just three years ago Martha Louise had been born, and someone labelled her the Hallelujah! baby. Not a misnomer that, because the one thing my orthopaedic surgeon had strongly advised after thorough examination and myelogram of my degenerative spine was, "No more children." And so it might have been had the Lord not seen fit to heal my back in November of 1964. Martha Louise was born in June 1965, by normal delivery following an easy labour.

"Tell you what," Graham was saying. "Why don't you go up to bed for a while and take it easy. I'll ring Joe and see what he thinks."

Dear Joe. Friend and doctor. We had seen him just yesterday when we returned from a weekend of ministry in Louisiana. The new Eastway General Hospital, where I would be going in a month's time, had officially opened on that Sunday. Joe had encouraged us to drop in for the open house and, since the hospital was located close to the freeway on our way home, we decided to do just that.

Sprawled out over spacious grounds due east of the city, the hospital had in every detail that 'just finished' look, with sparkling corridors, colourfully decorated private rooms complete with television, newly-seeded lawn and sprinkler system. There was as yet no antiseptic smell, and the whole aspect of the place was á la motel.

How pleasant it would be to check in here for a few days rest, I thought, never dreaming how soon I would have the chance.

The nursery was of particular interest: only a few baby beds were visible and when I queried one of the attendants, she explained that Monday would be the first functioning day for the hospital, and the babies would be transported — in their tiny beds — from the old hospital to the new.

The picture of the bare, unfurnished nursery floated back into my mind at intervals during the day, and the mild contractions continued at intervals too. I recalled having 'false labour' with our second child and compared the two. Definitely not the same, I thought.

"Joe says just to stay in bed. You're probably overtired from the weekend's trip, and need to get off your feet for a while." Graham was on his way to the church. "See you a bit later."

It's too early, Lord.

As if he didn't know. I mean — really, he arranged the whole thing, hung the moon, put the stars in their orbit and figured out how long it takes to make babies. Who am I to tell him? Still, it helped just to share my thoughts with him that way, and he didn't seem to be laughing back. On the contrary, a deep peace settled over me as the day progressed and I knew I was not to worry. "Our times are in his hands," the Psalmist reminded me.

Myra's visit helped too. She was a friend in the parish, a nurse, and her very presence seemed to reassure me.

Certainly there was a lot I could have worried about. For example the hospital costs. Our new lifestyle of barely four years' duration made no provision for savings to meet this kind of need. But hadn't the Lord assured us that if we would be about his kingdom's business full-time, he would be about the business of looking after us . . . full-time? The memory of cancelling those insurance policies was still vivid, and this circumstance would appear to be a 'crunch' or a test of some kind. And yet in the heat of the fray, I never gave it a moment's thought.

Really a bit out of character for me, I thought as I reflected on these events later, *not to worry at all. After all, I had spent some of the best years of my life anxiously contriving how to make ends meet. By now it was like a conditioned response. Was the Lord really changing me? Changing an attitude so basic that it seemed almost a part of my personality?*

The drive to the hospital was uneventful. *The stars at*

night really are bright here in the heart of Texas, I mused, glancing out of the car windows. Away from the hazy, smoggy air of East End, out here in the cool, night-bright countryside, how big the stars seemed, and how close to heaven we seemed in consequence.

Only after I had checked into the obstetric ward and was safely inside a labour room did the newness of the hospital become apparent.

"I'll be with you in a minute," the night nurse called around the corner from the corridor. "I can't seem to find the light switch."

Five seconds passed . . . ten . . .

"There! That's better. This is our first night working here, you know, so we have to locate a few things."

A few things, indeed! I certainly hope . . .

"Just lie here," she continued, "and I'll elevate your head a bit."

She gave several good turns to a knob under the table, and my feet began to rise.

The nurse paused, looking slightly embarrassed. "Well, let's try that once again," she laughed, returning my feet to a level position and trying a different knob. "We'll get things working here sooner or later," she smiled reassuringly.

Well — certain things definitely are working, I thought to myself as another hard contraction came, *and it would be convenient for certain other things to be working by the time they are needed!*

Graham sat and read a book. Once he stepped outside. He came back chuckling.

"They can't find the soap."

We looked at each other and then we both laughed. I

remembered a scene in that epic film, *Gone With the Wind*, when Miz Scarlett was in labour. All the servants were running hither and yon to fetch things and Prissy kept screeching for 'More hot water!' The surroundings were very different, but there was the same flurry of excitement. The peace was there, however. Somehow I knew they would find the soap and it would be all right.

At seven in the morning a baby boy was born, and my work was done. At least for now. We named him David, for the shepherd boy who loved to sing and play to the Lord, and Earle for our dear friend and teacher Earle Frid, a man who had taught us how to take God at his word — simply and trustingly.

As soon as Graham had seen the baby he came into my room.

"I just had an interesting conversation at the nursery window," he reported.

Oh yes, the bare nursery, I remembered.

"A lady was there looking through the window at her grandchild who was born just a few minutes after David, and she said to me, 'So you're the lucky one!' I was a little puzzled, so I asked her what she meant. And she said (here Graham paused and his eyes were twinkling merrily) "Well, of course the first baby born in the new hospital is on the house."

"On the house?" I interjected.

"Yes, that's what she said. The hospital pays all his expenses."

The words sank in deeply, and I could see in Graham's face the joy of a man who had waited patiently on the Lord.

"Not only that, but do you know what else?"

"I can't imagine."

"Joe says he checks out to be a full-term baby. I mean, he's not in any sense premature."

"Well . . ."

We both laughed.

"I guess the Lord just ripened him up in a hurry so he could take advantage of this free offer!"

We laughed again.

"Now, can you think of anything cleverer than that — I mean, if you were God and looking around for ways to pay our hospital bills, could you in a million years think of a cleverer plan than that?" I asked.

We laughed again.

9

The House on North Main Street

The sultry night air was heavy with a blended stench of coal dust and diesel fumes. Cars zoomed in and out of the tunnel, radios blaring. I sat on the front steps and pondered. *It's not a home I would ever have chosen, that's for sure.*

To my right, fifty yards away and directly over the tunnel, began the maze of railroad tracks; not exactly a choice playground for children, but it held a certain fascination for ten-year-old Nathan. He and Cracken loved to go berry picking in all the brambles near the tracks, and had produced the makings of several fine fruit pies that way. Cracken was my age, still a tomboy at heart, and a perfect companion for Nathan on these escapades. I smiled when I remembered their last excursion. They had wandered in different directions with their berry baskets until a policeman stopped Cracken, warning her that it was not safe for them to be there alone. It was Nathan who reported the incident:

"Humph! I don't see why the policeman said that." His tousled red hair partially concealed a furrowed brow, and he seemed to be sensing that his happy hours playing on the tracks were numbered. "There's nothing dangerous out there."

"Oh?" I waited for an explanation.

"There's nobody out there except some old winos," he went on.

"Indeed!" My eyebrows rose quite of their own accord.

"Yes. They're just ..." Nathan paused, his freckled nose wrinkling to find the right word, "they're just regular old men."

Regular indeed. His acceptance of them was so transparent that I had not known what to say next.

Behind the house was a trucking company whence emanated the diesel fumes. The loading and unloading took place in the small hours of the morning, and the diesel din became a familiar night noise, as the song of crickets had once been in the suburbs. *I'll never take silence for granted again — or fresh air.*

*   *   *

To my left ran a narrow side street, where the heavy tandem trucks pulled out and applied their airbrakes at the corner, then assaulted the early morning stillness in low gear as they turned north, heading towards the freeway. Beyond was an empty lot, and half a block away one of Houston's most notorious nightclubs. Seldom, if ever, did Saturday night pass without gunshots ringing out through the darkness. In front of me ran North Main Street and on the other side of it a deserted house. *How did we ever come to be here*, I asked myself.

T–MS–C

I knew the answer, of course. First there had been an unexpected caller at the rectory. Her name was Victoria Booth Demarest, and in the tradition of her illustrious forebears, who had 'tread the city's streets again' and established that remarkable arm of evangelism and mercy known as the Salvation Army, she had turned our eyes towards the wandering youth of the city, and opened our hearts to the hippie crowd. She herself was an almost eighty-year-old hippie, whose manner and dress expressed the flamboyance of her personality and paid no homage to the clichés of fashion. She captivated our imagination.

The Lord had done so much to bring peace and order into our lives. And we had had to pay, as individuals, a very high price for that kind of corporate cohesion. Our lives as we had known them had been pulled apart — the habits, daily routines, and perichant for privacy, the looking after 'your own' — and painfully put back together again, with our feet set in a larger place, our vision expanded, our hearts enlarged to receive one another as dearly beloved brethren. Surely the Lord was not asking us to forsake this hard-won unity and expose our lives to the ravages of a rootless, disoriented sub-culture group?

Surely he was. But not as a forsaking of what had been, as I had first feared. More as a fulfilment. Was it because of what had been that the Lord was able to call us to this new ministry in the heaving heart of the city? I pondered.

The traffic hum subsided, and a summer breeze stirred the boughs of the sycamores. I slid my thumb and forefinger down the smooth, cool length of an iris leaf. Remembering the first time I ever saw the house, I could still hear the tyres grating to a halt on the gravel and Graham saying, "Let's see if old Mr. Valdez is at home."

A notary public, he was the sole occupant of the rambling two-storey frame house on the corner. In better days it had served as a chiropractic clinic, and in still better, a comfortable family residence in the twenties. Now it was a flop house.

The five of us had piled out of the car: Graham, Arabella, Bill, Nancy and myself — all the adults in our rectory household. And sure enough, Mr. Valdez was home.

Walking up these steps was very hard for me, I recall. My body moved slowly, heavily, part corpse — part balking mule. And once inside the dimly-lit hallway, I heard Arabella's voice.

"Graham! Look! This room . . ." she motioned towards a parlour-like room on our left, with large bay window and window seat against the far wall.

"It's just like the one in my dream!" she continued.

Through my numbness I recalled a dream Arabella had shared with us, in which Annie, a gifted young musician in the church, was sitting near a window singing and playing a guitar.

"It was this very room," she exclaimed with an excitement too obvious to deny but too dangerous to share it. The very thought of uprooting our lives to move into such a place as this was unthinkable. Was it possible that Arabella's 'vision' could actually change the way we lived and where we did it? And why was Graham so open to her dreams and visions and so unresponsive to my practical, sensible way of looking at things?

The inner struggle continued as we walked through the remainder of the house. I recoiled at the dirt, the grime, the peeling plaster which at several points erupted violently into big gaping holes in the ceiling, the floorboards through which you could see the ground beneath. *It was not a bad home in its day,* I thought. *It's sad to see a house so forsaken, so ruined.*

Then we came to the garage. The filth was more concentrated here, the decay more obvious. Yet as Arabella and Graham began to talk, it was as if we might have been standing in a Disney wonderland.

"Can't you just see it? It would be a wonderful spot for a coffee-house."

"Look! You could use this area for a refreshment bar."

"Say, this would be an ideal spot for a stage." My four friends were wandering hopefully about, examining the entire garage while I stood stockstill in one corner, my eyes roaming over the debris. *I must have my channels mixed. Can they possibly be serious?*

The street had gone very quiet now. I could hear the faint rustling of sycamore leaves. *Yes, that was my first introduction to North Main.* My next thought was awesome. *And my friends were right. That old garage is a coffee-house now.* I pondered for a moment. *And I was there when faith believed it.*

The air seemed clearer, the streetlight brighter, and my thoughts sharper. *Not my faith. Theirs ... not theirs either. It was the faith of the Son of God himself, available to those who do not stumble over their own comfort and fall short of seeing his kingdom's plan.*

My friends could see it. And I could see them seeing it. And I followed ... haltingly.

10

"Next week's the time we need to move."

"Next week!?" I stared at Graham in utter disbelief. "But the kitchen's barely finished and there's no wiring for the washer and dryer yet."

"We can attend to all those details once we're moved in at North Main."

I stared at him coldly. Details, indeed. With a baby in the house, the washing machine and dryer were more like a lifeline than a 'detail'. Sometimes I could not for the life of me determine what made this man tick.

"Surely one more week will not make all that difference," I pleaded. But I could feel the wheels rolling.

That was on Wednesday. Moving day was set for Monday. For the next two days my soul wore blue pyjamas, barely rousing from a depressive somnolence to move about, fry the eggs, answer the phone, summon a smile to send the children off and welcome them home from school.

Why am I such a stick in the mud? But there it is: a stick in the mud I am. O Lord, please get me unstuck. For without you I can do no good thing.

The eggs were frying and it was Friday morning. Or were they frying? I gazed at the jelly-liquid state of our farm fresh eggs lying in the pan. No, they were definitely not frying. They were definitely just lying in there. Mostly uncooked.

"Whatever is the matter with this burner?" I murmured to myself just as Nancy walked through the kitchen door.

"I don't know. It was working last night when I heated the kettle," she answered, peering over my shoulder.

The family was assembling in the dining-room as I moved the frying pan to another burner. Hopefully this one was working.

"Mother, you know that load of clothes you put in first thing this morning?" Mary asked from the next room. "They're still just scooching around in the machine. I think the agitator must be broken."

"Just pull the knob and turn it off," I called over my shoulder, trying to keep an eye on the toast and not burn it, for once. "I'll see about it later."

At ten o'clock I finished wringing out the last piece of laundry by hand and, with a sigh, tossed the clothes into the dryer, turning the dial.

The telephone was ringing; it was Eloise about the P.T.A. board position.

"Yes, well, no we're not leaving the church. We're leaving the rectory . . . but it will be very difficult for me to make regular meetings because of our living across town. That's why I wanted you to ring. I just don't think it's practical for me to be on the board this year."

72

The day's ceaseless round moved on. Soon it was lunch-time, and Arabella was returning from the church.

"Hi. It was a good morning; lots of people for Bible Sharing. I'd say two dozen easily."

"Sounds like two sharing groups."

"Could be. There would certainly be opportunity for a lot more participation if the group was smaller." She disappeared into the laundry room, and I could hear her slightly muffled voice calling me.

"Did you just put these clothes in the dryer?"

"Heavens, no. It was at least two hours ago. Are they still going?"

"Hmm." There was a long pause and I could hear the door shut and the humming sound of the dryer resume. Arabella stepped out of the laundry room and now I could hear her better.

"If you ask me, I think the heating element is gone. It makes a noise and the drum moves around, but there's no heat."

Somewhere bells rang. Faintly. And then I had a thought. *First it was the stove, then the washing machine, and now the dryer. The very things I was insisting on having before we move.*

I was beginning to smile inwardly if not outwardly. *It's outrageous.*

I was laughing out loud now.

Yes, I know that you have power to make streams spring up in the desert, and to dry up rivers, to provide appliances in our new home, and turn off appliances in our old one! I really hear you talking, Lord.

Thank you.

And that's how the stick in the mud got unstuck.

11

The
Way
In

"Sh! This way, children." I tugged at Martha's sleeve with my free hand while carrying David in my other arm, a diaper bag swinging from my shoulder.

"Can't we just . . ."

"No, Jane, we can't." Her eyes wandered wistfully to the garden beyond as we turned to go up the front steps. Her feet dawdled. "You remember what Daddy said. It's opening night at the coffee-house and he doesn't want us around." I caught her eye and smiled playfully. "Not that we're not nice to have around, you understand. It's just that coffee-houses and children don't mix. Up you go."

We climbed the steps and went inside. It was just like any other Friday night. We had all (except the cats) gone to the weekly meeting at the church, driving across Houston's industrial middle to the East End and back again. How strange it seemed, even after all those months, not to be able to dash over from the rectory next door.

There was something different about tonight, however.

74

Months of hard work and 'live-in' preparation, training in street evangelism for some, and prayer by all had gone into this grand opening. No wonder footsteps quickened and there was an air of excitement as we entered the house on this warm summer evening.

July 4, 1969 — a date to remember, I thought. Then I had another thought.

"I'll tell you what, kids. You go up and get your pyjamas on, and after I put David to bed, we'll have a special surprise."

Footsteps sounded on the steep stairs and faded into the sitting-room above. I paused in the kitchen to rinse out the baby bottles, and then began the slow ascent with David's sleepy head jogging against my shoulder. I was remembering the night (Could it have been only a week ago?) when we sat on these same stairs, some sitting along the wall of the wide hallway and some spilling over into the living-room. We had gathered together to decide on a name for the coffee-house. There was a sober excitement about it all. After singing a few songs, the eleven who had recently gone to New York shared some of their experiences in street evangelism, and afterwards we began to think seriously about the name. We spoke quietly to one another about our Father's faithfulness to us in this place, the wonder and the depth of his life which he was showing us daily as we worshipped together, the strong reality of his Son Jesus in the midst of us. Now what had all this to do with the multitudes outside North Main Street?

In my mind's eye I could see the tunnel in front of the house, and cars streaming out of the dark abyss. Somehow it seemed symbolic.

"The way out," I mused, half aloud.

There was a pause, and Bill turned his head thoughtfully.

"The Way In," he said simply.

The way in.

Yes, that was it.

The way into a new life — of sharing, of caring. Daring to live in radical adventuresome ways to bring in his kingdom.

The Way In. Yes. It was the right name for the coffee-house, no doubt of it at all.

*   *   *

David snuggled into his familiar crib and I closed the door quietly. In the sitting-room Jane and Martha waited dutifully in their pyjamas, all a'twitter with excitement.

"What's the surprise?" they asked with shining eyes.

"The surprise is ... Let's see your teeth. Are they brushed?"

A chorus of 'umm' assured me they were.

"The surprise is waiting inside my room. Now, it's going to be quite dark, so take my hand."

Off went the lights, and I led the small procession of pyjama-clad figures towards the big double windows directly over the entrance to the garage-turned-coffee-house.

Soft strains of guitar music floated towards us, and we could hear Mimi singing.

"Now, if you'll be very quiet, I'll raise the blinds so you can see all the people at the coffee-house." Soft shudders of excitement were in the air as the blinds came up slowly. Below us spread the side lawn of the North Main house, framed with sycamore and tallow trees. Colourful round-top tables dotted the lawn (commercial cable spools which had been donated, then painted) and a striped green and white awning announced the garage entrance to The Way In.

At first the floodlit lawn and its attractive appointments captured my attention and prevented my noticing how few people there were. Now I strained to see into the night shadows. The music had stopped and that meant one of the entertainment 'sets' was over. Soon people would be streaming outside to enjoy their refreshments on the lawn. Hard as I tried, I could not see a single unfamiliar face. What had I expected on opening night? A throng? A dozen or so? I was grappling with my own sense of disappointment when Jane tugged at my sleeve and whispered, "Mommie, look! There's a hippie!"

I followed her finger to the far edge of the lawn, and sure enough, there was a young man in jeans and a partially buttoned sports shirt leaning against one of the spool tables. Hippie or not, he was definitely a young man whom I had not seen before.

But where are all the others?

The others? Scattered all around the globe they were, if I had but known, and many of them didn't wear blue jeans or have long hair. Many of them sat in church pews waiting for the revelation that God has a family for us to live in, a place where we can live and move and have our being transformed daily. For the revelation that God wants to grow us up, not simply stamp us 'SAVED'. We were to have an exciting part in the renewing work of God's Spirit in his church.

But first there was a work to do among us, a work that had already begun, and to which a new ingredient was added that very night. Were we really willing to roof this old house, renovate the interior, turn our lives upside down, inside out, and suffer the inconveniences of this not-so-nice neighbourhood for the sake of one tousled-haired youth? I glanced outside at the boy again. Or did we have something better in mind? Something more successful? Were we willing simply to be planted in this place, and leave the sprouting of the seed and the flourishing of the fruit to the Lord?

From this tiny seed and inauspicious beginning grew a worldwide ministry of renewal in the Lord's church. Here, at The Way In, the Fisherfolk* ministry had its birth.

---

* A team of young adults who travel as part of the outreach ministry of the Community of Celebration.

12

Divine Décor

Two visitors stood in the new rectory hallway: I hadn't seen Bernice and Elaine for years. We had been good friends when we all lived in Galveston years ago.

"Yes, of course I have time, and I'm delighted you found us!" I said almost automatically, though not insincerely. I really was glad to see them, even though life in the new rectory was as busy as it had ever been in the one next door to the church. "Would you like to see a bit of the house?" *How to explain the changes in our life? Where do I even begin?*

"Let me take your coats. Now, let's see. You came in the back way, didn't you? So you've seen the kitchen. I go in twenty times a day just to gaze at those beautiful twin wall-ovens. They were just installed, and I have to pinch myself to believe they're really here. They make cooking for a family of twenty much, much easier."

"Twenty!" echoed Bernice.

"Yes. Does that seem a lot? I guess it would have to me a couple of years ago." *Would it ever ... did it ever! I'll never forget the day in the downstairs hall at the North Main house — not nearly so nice a downstairs hall as this — when my thoughts screamed out to the Lord, 'I can't love twenty people all at once!' And as I stood frozen in my own exasperation and defeat, the Lord spoke to my thoughts. 'Very well,' he said, 'try loving just one at a time. Try loving the person you're face to face with now.' I looked up into the face of one of his dear saints, and I was suddenly freed from the burden of numbers ... free to love ... one at a time ... hour by hour ... day by day.*

We were entering the dining-room. "Lovely!" I heard Elaine exclaim. "Is this your own furniture? I mean, when you live together this way, I really don't understand how it works ... how you ..." she fumbled for words.

I nodded my understanding. "Well, I'll tell you about it, since you asked specifically about this room. It has quite a story to tell, in fact. Not too flattering to me ..." I shrugged. "Oh well ...

"For several years our household had been expanding, but mostly they were single people who brought along a few suitcases, a trunk of clothing perhaps, a record player, but with Virginia it was different."

"Oh?"

"She had four children for one thing. And a houseful of furniture for another." I could smile as I remembered the whole situation, but at the time it had been no laughing matter. "One day before she moved in, we sat down,

80

Graham and Virginia and I, to discuss how we would accommodate our new enlarged family at mealtimes. Virginia had some high-backed, narrow dining-room chairs which used much less space than ours. The table could seat many more people if we used them. There was every good reason to do so. But suddenly my thoughts boiled up inside. 'But I like OUR chairs . . . after all, it's OUR house . . .' "

"Well, isn't it?" Elaine interjected.

"No." I was surprised by the interruption. "Actually the church owns it. We've never had a home of our own. But that's beside the point, really; the point being that when we had committed ourselves to sharing our home with another family, suddenly I was faced with my emotional attachment to our chairs, and there it was, plain as day . . . big four-legged pieces of wood. I can chuckle about it now, and I love the way this room looks with those high-backed chairs, but I guess that's because I learned to love the people who sat in them!"

We strolled into the living-room and sat down. The conversation turned towards the past, as I enquired about the ages and whereabouts of Bernice's children, and about Elaine's elderly mother. Pretty soon Elaine chuckled, "Now, you're going to think I have a one-track brain, to keep coming back to the same subject. But this really intrigues me. What I want to know is . . . whose furniture is in this room?"

I laughed. "It's a real mixture, I can tell you. That piece beside the door is an old oak washstand which Graham refinished years ago. He discovered it in my mother's basement when we were first married." I smiled, remembering how it had looked back in those days. "It was one of our first period pieces. We painted everything with black

81

lacquer in those days. I can't recall who has described that period as Early Married Oriental!"

"Well, it's a gorgeous thing now," Elaine said. "I've never seen such unusual brass pulls."

"They were part of the ornamentation on an old sewing machine Graham rescued from the basement of St. David's Church."

"Does he spend all his time in old basements?"

"No," I laughed, "not exactly. Oh yes, those wood inlay panels came from the sewing machine too."

"Remarkable."

"I think so. The bevelled piece across the back was an afterthought — to cover up the place where the towel bar used to be."

"My, he thinks of everything, doesn't he?"

"Yes. He likes to salvage and restore things. And people," I added reflectively, for, with God's help it was true.

"This piano belonged to Arabella, the young woman you met when you came in. We restored it to the natural wood finish. And the sofa and tables came from Dr. Bob's home in Alta Loma. He's our doctor friend who is serving the Lord in many remarkable ways here. One of his favourite hobbies is giving away houses or leaving them behind to go where God calls him."

"You do have some adventurous new friends," Bernice commented wryly.

"I guess adventure is one of the keynotes of our life these days. It was a real adventure moving into this house, I can tell you. We had been living at North Main, where The Way In coffee-house was begun. Many young adults moved in to be a part of that outreach ministry, and pretty soon our family was no longer needed there. But our furniture was! At least, quite a bit of it. We arrived here with Arabella's piano and one chair to furnish this vast living-room.

"It wasn't too bad, because we were planning to have meetings of university students in this room, so there would certainly be lots of space for people to sit on the floor!" Elaine looked amused.

"However, we discovered one major drawback on the day before the first meeting. There were no overhead lights in the room, only floor plugs — numerous floor plugs — (the original owner of the house was also its builder and he had spared no effort to equip the house lavishly). Our problem was: we had no lamps! We had been far too busy settling into this fine house to fret over such little details, but suddenly I began to wonder if we would hold our evening meeting by candlelight."

"And did you?" Elaine was keenly on the edge of this conversation.

"No. But you'll never guess why not. The day before the meeting, who should drive up but the Gwens. They are the couple who previously lived here, if you can imagine a couple rattling around in this big house! They carried a tall table lamp, explaining that it just didn't fit into their tiny new apartment. Would we be interested? And of course . . ."

"And of course you said, 'yes'."

"Well, of course."

Elaine shook her head wonderingly.

"So we did have light for the prayer meeting . . . and not many weeks afterwards the other furniture came from Dr. Bob's house. And *voilà* — a lovely living-room, just made to order!"

"It sounds so simple the way you tell it," Elaine said.

"It was simple . . . very simple," I said. Then a funny thought struck me, and I added, "Simply divine."

13

Where
thieves
break
through

In the early morning stillness I sat reading, and pondering, still snugly wrapped in bed covers.

Behold, he that keepeth Israel neither slumbers nor sleeps. What a comforting psalm it was, and especially then, when Graham and Bill were travelling and away from us so much of the time; it was good to be reminded that the Lord's watchful care never ceased by day or by night.

I closed my eyes and relaxed in the peace of his presence, with a sense of security. Moments passed. I cannot tell how long I had lain there when a bustling sound below me let me know that the household had risen. As I put on my robe and slippers I heard Cracken's voice. Did I detect a note of alarm? My footsteps quickened along the upstairs hallway until I met Cracken face to face on the stairs.

"There's been a burglary," she said, slightly out of breath, her dark eyes flashing. "Don't know what they took yet, but I found something they left behind."

I followed her into the panelled den and saw it: there, sitting at an angle on the sofa, was the television set.

Our glances met.

"How strange."

"I'm guessing he just left it when he heard me running the shower — I got up real early to take one. Funny. I stopped at the bathroom door because I thought I heard a noise downstairs, but then there was nothing so I went ahead and took my shower." Cracken was applying her best detective-logic to the situation. "I'm sure he heard me and got scared and ran."

By now there were lots of young junior detectives roaming the house in search of clues.

"Aunt Betty!" Anna called from the dining-room. "Come look!"

She was pointing to the handsome Early American break-front against the far wall.

"The spoons!"

The row of antique silver berry spoons which had hung from the spoon rack had completely vanished from sight.

"Oh," my heart sank. "Well, now, let's keep looking to see if there's anything else missing."

But there was nothing. It soon became apparent that the thief had barely begun his exploits before he was startled away by Cracken's trip to the bathroom.

"It's good Cracken decided to take a shower," said Carl with his wry smile.

"Yes, it is," I answered. "You know, I thought of something else that's good. I'll tell you at breakfast."

The ordinariness of breakfast preparations relieved the trauma of our rising and soon we were gathered around that most comforting place, the family dining table, where I shared the psalm I had read earlier, a psalm which suddenly took on a new depth of meaning.

"He that keepeth thee neither slumbers nor sleeps."

"Now I reckon . . ." the children were gazing steadily at me, "that means the Lord knew everything that was going on here, and was completely in charge of it. Do you think that's what it means?"

Various nods and soft assenting sounds answered me.

"That's good news, isn't it?" Cracken's merry twinkle had returned and relaxed the lines of her face.

"I can't get over the Lord having me read that particular psalm. I mean, I could have read about Cain killing Abel or Shemida begetting Sheckem, or . . ."

The children were beginning to smile.

" — or the ten 'mandments," said wee David.

"Yes, I could certainly have read those. They're always helpful. It just seems . . ." I paused to contemplate, "it just seems that the Lord wanted us to know he was awake and watching this whole episode, and so, not to worry."

Thank you, Lord, for sending your word to guide, to comfort, to cheer us.

I watched the children peacefully leave the table and get themselves ready for school.

The morning went smoothly and at noon Cathleen returned from her design work in The Fishermen office.

"Oh, by the way, I saw Sylvia at sharing this morning, and she sent a message to you."

"Oh, what?"

"Well, it was one of those funny things. I was telling her about our burglary, you know, and about all the silver berry spoons getting stolen, and . . ."

"Yes. Go on."

"Well, Sylvia said — " Cathleen's soft features were half-quizzical, her voice warm and gentle. "Now this is what she said — she said it just like this — she said, 'You tell Betty Jane not to worry. She'll get those berry spoons back.' "

She'll do what?

The first part sounded familiar; the Lord had surely told us not to worry. But getting the berry spoons back? It hadn't even occurred to me to think of it, ask it, or expect it.

I smiled and gave a little shrug. "Well, that's a new thought. Mind you, it doesn't sound too likely under the circumstances, but we'll take it as a word of encouragement anyway!" In my mind's eye I could see Sylvia's wonderful open face, a face that radiated the simplicity of her trust in God.

We're really very fortunate to have lost only a handful of berry spoons, when you come right down to it. My thoughts returned to conversations with several of our neighbours about the high incidence of theft in the area, a problem heightened by racial tensions in this part of the city. Our next door neighbours, both professional people, had had all of their family silver stolen while they were away at work. Finally, they had resorted to a burglar alarm system, a watchdog, and double locks on all their doors. Even with this protection they seemed disheartened and depressed about the situation. I remembered telling them (hopefully to encourage), of the Lord's faithfulness to us at the North Main House, a house which was impossible to lock, located in a 'high-crime' district, a house protected by the Lord alone. I couldn't help pondering how our present affluent neighbourhood seemed besieged by thievery problems, while houses in the North Main area had gone unnoticed by the most enterprising burglars.

Oh, yes, the afternoon jobs. A glance at the clock reminded me that it was almost time to fetch the children from school. Each day there were simple afternoon chores for them to do: sweeping the carport or raking leaves or mowing a part of the spacious lawn. Since ten of them arrived home at once, it was a great advantage to think things through ahead of time! *Let's see: Carl can sweep the carport, and Martha can help; then there's the side lawn to mow* — pretty soon it was sorted out reasonably well, though there were times when I wished for a computerised brain.

An hour later I watched from the kitchen window as our junior grounds crew flew into action, if you can call their languid southern tempo 'flying'. I smiled at the thought of my first employer, a man from Michigan, who maintained the air-conditioning in our building at an unswerving 60° because 'the only way you can get any work out of Southerners is to half freeze them to death!'

Watching the children provided an interesting study in human work habits. There were several real beavers, who worked briskly to get their chores done, even though thoroughness might be wanting. Then a few always managed to make a game of the most onerous task (the really creative ones?): one day it might be a leaf-fight, the next a balancing act with the rake on top of their heads. Others had internalised the 'Lazy-bones sleepin' in the sun' ethos to the point of a real science: for every two sweeps of the broom they would stop and lean on the broom handle for twenty seconds. The distant drone of the lawnmower was comforting; at least it was running today, and the jobs which were out of sight were not out of mind!

The work had been going on for twenty minutes when

the lawnmower crescendoed to an intense forte just outside the kitchen, and Bill stuck his head in the screened door and shouted over the din, "Look, Mom."

His lean, six-foot form filled the doorway, and he was grinning and wiping the sweat from his brow with the sleeve of his T-shirt.

"See what I found?"

I looked.

"They were just lying there by the tree trunk." He was pointing to the slender tallow tree near the street. "I saw something shining and, well, here they are!"

He thrust a big fistful of slightly dirty, grass-speckled silver berry spoons into my hand.

"Praise God," I exclaimed without a moment's hesitation. "Look, everybody, look, children. The berry spoons! Just like Sylvia said, they're back."

"Well, I never . . ."

"Did he just leave them there?"

All in one day, I thought. *A word of wisdom from the Lord, a burglary, a prophecy and its fulfilment. O Lord, thank you for speaking to that young thief about who you are and what you want. Thank you for being our keeper. Thank you that we can go to sleep in great peace, leaving our lives and those we love and all that we have in the strong arms of your keeping.*

14

Culture Shock

Three faw uh dime!
Hav' uh good time!
Lookie, lookie,
Who's got de cookie?

E'erbody faw de cake wawk go dis way.

The din of noise bombarded my eardrums and set up a
high humming sound inside my head. *What on earth am I
doing here,* something inside me said. *What is a nice girl
like me ... doing in a place ... like this?* My head knew
what I was doing here. I was doing my duty to God and my
country by attending the school carnival. Of course. There
was no doubt in my mind that I should be here. I had even
served on one of the carnival committees. *Then why do I*

feel like screaming inside? I walked down the hallway of Lockhart Elementary School, and I was appalled to see well-equipped classrooms converted into sopping wet sponge throw areas, sticky candy apple dispensaries, noisy queues for dart games. *This should be going on outside, in the playground. School buildings were not made for this kind of abuse.* My Anglo-Saxon mentality kept telling me things, and something strong inside me wanted to bolt and run. I was experiencing a kind of culture shock, and slowly I recognised it for what it was.

The autumn before our children had started attending Lockhart School. They and a handful of other students were the only white faces to be seen at this ninety-five per cent black-American school. The junior and senior high schools had even fewer white students – about two per cent. Having heard all our lives about minority groups, we were now having the opportunity to be one. The autumn of 1970 was the first time that legal teeth had been put into the integration of Houston's public schools. Feelings were running high and there had been considerable speculation about how many children from our affluent neighbourhood would show up for registration at the schools into which they had been zoned. Many did not. Some families enjoyed the luxury of private or parochial schools for their children. Others sold their homes and moved, creating a near-panic situation with real estate in the area. Still others rented apartments elsewhere in the city, establishing a legal residence for themselves while maintaining their home as well, and thus circumventing the law.

Two days before school opened my telephone rang and the voice on the other end of the line was Edith MacNeill's. "I was just thinking," she said, "how good it would be to get together on the first day of school and pray for our children in their new school situations."

"What a good idea!" I said, not realising that the outcome would be a weekly prayer meeting in our home. But so it was. As the five of us — all from the University Oaks neighbourhood, and all with children in the area schools — sat and prayed that Monday morning, I kept remembering seven-year-old Jane. I had chauffeured the children to school that first day and walked with Jane down the hall to find her second-grade classroom. She was fine until we stood together on the threshold of the room and she gazed at a sea of friendly black faces. I felt her body stiffen against mine, her hand gripping my hand as she whispered tautly, "Mother, I can't go in."

"Of course you can, honey," I began, and talked to her quietly. In a few minutes she did go in timorously, reluctantly. As I drove home I could still hear her words and feel her hand gripping mine: *I can't go in.* She didn't say 'I don't want to go in', or 'I'm afraid to go in', or 'I won't go in'. She said *I can't go in, my legs won't take me; I am paralysed by the shock of all these others who look different from me.*

That afternoon a new Jane emerged — happy and chatty, telling us all about the wonderful first day she had had at school; how all the children wanted to stroke her hair — 'It's so smooth!', carry her books, help her in every way possible. Instead of a woeful misfit she had feared herself to be, she seemed more like queen for the day. *Thank you, Lord.*

As I stood in the middle of this carnival atmosphere, I could better understand Jane's experience that Monday morning than I ever had before. But here it was, a year later, and of course I was a big girl. My problem was not so much the paralysis of fear; it was rather the unexplainable numbness of a situation that should feel familiar but doesn't. I had been to dozens of Halloween carnivals, but this one lacked the decorum which upper middle-class Anglo-Saxons seem to summon at church and school functions. I have since experienced similar nonplussing situations: at the supermarket check-out counter in England when I realised with a start that there were no double-strength paper sacks provided for the groceries, and I should have brought a shopping basket like all the English housewives; or at a small hotel in Norway, when, after a long and tedious day of driving, we were handed the room key by a pleasant non-English-speaking night clerk and suddenly twigged to the fact that our room was four double flights of steep stairs away. *How did I come to assume that the whole world had elevators?* Standing in the middle of the playground, I was aware of a free-wheeling, jostling and noisy environment that made me feel insecure.

Nor was I trapped in some petty prejudice against black Americans. Black people had been a part of my life always. As a pre-adolescent, my confidante had been a twenty-year-old Negress, who lived with her husband 'on the premises' of my parents' Southern home. She was a maid and more than a maid. She was a faithful friend, someone with whom I could share my best secrets. I loved her. No, the thing I was battling had to do with the corporate impact of an ethnic group; it had to do with feeling like a stranger in your own neighbourhood school. While I was reflecting about his, several boys from the school strolled up to where Nathan (my twelve-year-old son) and I were standing.

"Gimme ticke ..." came a thick-lipped request. The boy who made it was sullen and slight of stature.

I leaned forward and bent my ear towards him slightly. "I beg your pardon," I said, not having the faintest idea what he was trying to tell me.

"Gimme ticke ..." he reiterated, without the slightest change in his hostile drawl.

"I beg — "

Nathan broke in. "He's asking you for one of your carnival tickets," he said. I looked down and saw a half-dozen tickets in my left hand. We had purchased a lengthy roll of them when we had arrived half an hour before: the red ones sold for ten cents, the blue for twenty-five.

"How do you ask nicely for it?" I almost said to the boy. It was on the tip of my tongue when I stopped. Nathan stuffed his hand in his pocket and pulled out a red ticket. No words. With a slight toss of the head, he handed the ticket to the boy and shuffled his feet. The black boy made no audible response but darted off to the nearest concession stand.

Still pondering this rather strange turn of events (*Do I look unusually rich? ... unusually white, perhaps? ... are they the same?*) I was discussing with the children how much longer we could stay when what to my wondering eyes should appear but the same boy, back again.

"Gimme blue 'un ..."

Am I hearing correctly? Does he want a blue ticket now? Has he spent the red one already? Whereupon I spied it peeping out between his white thumbnail and black forefinger. He had brought it back.

I remembered now which stand he had made a beeline for, and my glance turned towards the sign which read

95

HOT DOGS 25¢. Slowly it sank into my consciousness. That was why he wanted the blue ticket. For the first time I had an opportunity to gaze deeply into the boy's eyes. They told me something I hadn't perceived before. They said, "I am hungry." Something relaxed deep inside me. Probably both his parents worked and that's why no adult was with him. Maybe they had forgotten to give him money to take to the carnival. Or maybe they had none to give him. In any event, I felt relieved and able to communicate.

I said, "You wanna buy a hot dog?"

He nodded. It took a blue one to do it, and I just happened to have one left.

*   *   *

At dinner that night the children were recounting their carnival exploits, comparing experiences and showing off their prizes.

"Tell them about the boy," I said to Nathan.

He looked thoughtful, then launched in. "Well, there were some boys who came up, and one of them asked Mama if he could please have a ticket."

He did what? I shook my head incredulously.

As the story continued, I heard, "And he came back and asked if he could please have a blue one."

He did??

I scarcely recognised the event that was being retold. But I recognised in the telling of it a kind of interpretation of tongues which I had never experienced before. The story was being told by a boy who, in much greater measure than I, had found out what it means to listen with an inner ear of understanding and to hear with the heart.

96

He was able to span the cultural gap and act as an interpreter. *Beauty*, I pondered, *is indeed in the eye of the beholder.*

"And a little child shall lead them."

15

Diary of a Pilgrim – Part 1

Tuesday, September 5, 1972:

David was lying with his head in my lap as the Dodge Sportsman van headed northeast, winding its way through Houston's spaghetti bowl. There was the impressive and familiar skyline, fully visible to me from my vantage point on the middle seat riding backwards.

I pondered.

Is there any similarity between me sitting on the back-facing seat, watching Houston's familiar landmarks receding into the slightly smoggy distance, and Lot's wife looking back at all the familiar scenes in Sodom as she left the city? I hope not.

I really *want* to go.

But there is no denying a curious emotional tug when I look at that skyline growing more distant by the moment.

Thank God for Abraham. For *somebody* who first had the guts to 'get thee from thy home and kindred, unto a land that I will show . . .' I can identify now. At one time I would have been terrified to go into such an unknown situation, leaving behind all that was familiar. But now – I looked at the faces of those who were with me in the van: I looked at Sherrell, at Anna, at Virginia, and down at David's fair head in my lap – now God has made us a family, in the fullness of that word. He has made us a group of people who can draw a strength from one another without possessing.

*　　*　　*

My thoughts flashed back to the first trip Graham made to England. How deeply that land impressed him, how the remembrance of it clung to him thereafter.

And those incredible invitations: one from an Anglican Bishop and another from a priest in his diocese (the left hand not knowing what the right was doing). And in essence the invitations were the same: "Can you come and help us?" The one gave us ecclesiastical sanction, the other a locality in which to work.

And then there was the airlines lady. For, even with ecclesiastical approval and a place to go, it would take a bit of doing to transport a household of eighteen across the Atlantic. One of God's coincidences allowed Graham to stay in the home of a Christian widow in Vancouver, B.C., during a ministry there, and as he shared his burden for England and his puzzlement at attempting to take such a large household so far away to live, she opened a curtain of hope for the future. Her husband had been an airlines official, and she had every confidence that special rates could be arranged for a group such as ours. A timely encouragement!

*　　*　　*

The Houston skyline was growing dimmer now. The

van ran so smoothly — not a bit like the tumultuous throbs and emotional jerks going on inside of me.

"I want to hold the string, Mama." It was David's voice.

"You want what?' I droned through my preoccupation.

"The string."

"Oh."

He is so fair, so beautiful lying there. So trusting.

"What string, David?"

Houston is the only home he has ever known. I wonder how it feels to be four and to experience this.

I glanced down and realised for the first time what David was talking about. A black ribbon marker dangled near his face, securely attached at the other end to a thin frayed New Testament which I was holding – a gift from our Bishop to Graham when he was ordained fifteen years ago.

"What do you want to do with the string?"

"I just want to hold on to it," came David's soft reply.

His innocent small fist closed over the string, his head resting against the Bible, and minutes later his eyes began to close too. A perfect picture of peace and trust. It made me smile.

I wonder if he knows — of course he can't possibly. But he must somehow.

As I looked at him – the long eyelashes, the upturned corners of his mouth, his absolutely relaxed, supple body, I was thinking how he represented us all.

In some sense we are all holding on to your string, O God.

We are holding on to that slender thread of chronology – of events and places, highways, airplane schedules, trains and ferries, which will lead us surely and steadily to the place you have told us to go.

Yes, Lord, we just want to hold on to your string.
We just want to hold on to your word.
We just want to hold on to you.

16

Diary of a Pilgrim - Part 2

Wednesday, September 6, 1972:

Last night in the motel the shower felt good, and mingled with it a shower of my salt-tears, tears of pain and separation, tears of grief.

We did it.

We really did it.

We left the place we love, the people we love, the church we love. We left them all.

All thy waves have gone over me, O God.

*   *   *

Both yesterday and today have been pleasant for travelling, surprisingly cool for Texas and Louisiana in early September. The sky was somewhat overcast and Sherrell remembered how the Lord had sent a cloud by day to shield his beloved people. We are his beloved people too. Amen and Hallelujah!

Leaving home is still a bit unreal. Occasionally I get a flashback of familiar faces, or a familiar place — like our family dining-room with its tall oak chairs around a large and slightly swaybacked table. It is hard to imagine that room empty at dinner time, but so it was last night.

Douglas has been doing a lot of driving. I've been thinking. We're not a very typical American family. The look on the night clerk's face when we registered in the motel last night was one of genuine puzzlement: three women and four girls in one room (with extra rollaway beds), and Douglas and the two little boys in the other room. I'm sure the night clerk had assumed that Douglas was married to at least one of us. Then when we gave her our names, she could tell we were a mixed breed, not bearing the same name or belonging to the same natural family, and her puzzlement showed.

Times like this always surprise me, because we don't seem odd to me. We seem like us, and it feels natural to be together. But I can understand the night clerk's problem. And I guess it would be a little less than obvious, even to some who know us, why I am travelling across-country with this nice young American priest and not with the one to whom I am married. I thought of Graham and Bill and the three teenage boys — two of Virginia's and one of ours — and wondered how they were faring on the southern route. We had left Houston at the same time, they to fulfil a ministry engagement, we to visit relatives in the Carolinas, rendezvousing with them in Fort Lauderdale before leaving the States. It sounded like a workable plan.

This noon we stopped at a state park in the heart of Mississippi. We found a lovely quiet place by a lake, with a picnic table and swings for children. Wading in the lake was fun too.

"I wonder if the lake has a name," I said to Douglas.

He mused. "Let's call it Lake Tohoomahatchee," he said, his brown eyes twinkling and his rich melodious laughter ringing out across the placid lake. "A good name," he continued, "for an anonymous lake."

"Oh . . . why?"

"Well, you know, so many Indian names end with 'ahatchee'. So," his eyes danced merrily, "To-whom-ahatchee . . .!"

"Oh really, Douglas." But none of us could help laughing. Laughter was a good kind of medicine for us too. Besides, Douglas's laughter had that wonderful contagious quality that always made you want to laugh with him.

More laughter. Then a lull, while we listened to the forest and lake sounds, the gentle lapping of waters, a distant bird call, a soft breeze through oak trees flocked with Spanish moss.

Tohoomahatchee, I mused.

By the water of Lake Tohoomahatchee we sat down.

We sat down and ate ham sandwiches.

We sat down.

And somewhere inside — in our inmost beings — we wept.

When we remembered you, O saints in Houston, whom we love.

*　　　*　　　*

This afternoon I was at the wheel. Glancing at the petrol gauge I saw the arrow was below the one-quarter mark.

Also, I was drowsy . . . no good when you are driving a ten-passenger vehicle. My thoughts said to the Lord, *It would be nice to find a service station and a place for refreshments.*

And there it was, scarcely two minutes down the highway, in the form of a Gulf station with a motel and coffee-shop. It was a Ramada Inn, quite new and luxurious. The others went ahead to order refreshments while I had the van serviced.

A few minutes later, as I entered the coffee-shop, I could see the children jumping excitedly and pointing to something on the wall.

"Look! See!" they cried. My eyes travelled from their joy-filled faces to a most amazing sight. Just above the booth where they were seated was a *very* familiar scene — the beautiful wallpaper mural from our dining-room in Houston, showing a magnificent old Southern mansion, not unlike the Houston rectory itself, and flooding our minds and hearts with memories.

"It's just like at home," Martha exploded. The children could not conceal their obvious delight.

Yes, it is just like home, I thought. *Here we are thirty-six hours away, sitting down at table together beside the same familiar picture. It's almost as if we had brought our dining-room with us, that dining-room where so many happy hours had been spent together.*

Do you suppose? Yes, it must be so. The Lord is showing us, in a most tender and loving way, that 'home' is going with us, just as surely as the cloud hovered over his children who were travelling through the wilderness.

He wants us to know that we are at home in him right

105

now. That he is going with us and we are going with him. That we are at home in him.

The presence of the cloud was close, protective, warm. Utterly secure.

17

Not a Sparrow Falls

The procession was making its way down the garden path, past the murmuring willows and nodding dahlias, round the curve by the saucer shape of the sometime pond. It was mid-May in Berkshire, and we were settling in the large manor house that had come to be our English home, thanks to the help of our friends, the Benedictine monks at Nashdom Abbey.

Springtime, the queen of seasons, was nowhere lovelier than the Berkshire downs. The lanes leading up to Yeldall Manor, ablaze with rhododendron, were variously lined with stately sequoias, and ample chestnuts. Formal rose gardens accented the front lawn where massive cedars, specimen trees from Ceylon and the Himalayas, spread their boughs in gentle supplication. The house itself had a storybook quality; it was of late Victorian vintage with mock-Tudor touches.

Just then the grounds had an especially well-manicured look, since the next day over a hundred guests would be coming to the reception following Arabella and Douglas's wedding in the parish church. Douglas was the young Episcopal clergyman who had come with us from America, and Arabella was one of the first Fisherfolk. Some of the guests had already arrived. Anna-Gretha Baumgren, colourfully attired in her Swedish national costume, had come all the way from Västeras, Sweden. And Sister Rosemary, an almost 80-year-old nun from Truro, was even now a part of an informal procession down the garden path on this balmy Friday afternoon as about a dozen of us gathered to attend the birdies' funeral.

*   *   *

Ba-ba and Hauker had come to live with us just three short weeks before. Expelled by accident and without warning from their tilting nest on the bough of a tree, the baby thrushes were soon discovered by the children and taken in for shelter, food and tender loving care. Their accommodation had presented some challenges from the start. First of all, there were three mature and worldly-wise cats who lived in the manor house along with their owners, English families there for a time of training in community leadership.

Then there was the matter of the frequent feedings necessary to sustain the life of the tiny birds. The first problem was adequately solved when a room in the cellar was earmarked 'for the birds'. The second was easily managed by Tricia, Martha and John during their spring holiday but when they returned to school things were more complex. At first the birdies went with them in a special box complete with the day's portions of milk-soaked bread. The teachers co-operated by allowing the children to dig up fresh worms at school. It was a demanding routine, and after several days what seemed like a simpler plan emerged: the grownups would take turns feeding them at home. Alas! The grownups, though willing, had many other household responsibilities, and on the second day, one of the feeding times was sadly forgotten and the birdies died.

The children were heartbroken. But their resilience was obvious almost immediately as they martialled all resources to plan a proper funeral for their feathered friends. They consulted Gary, who was of a liturgical bent, about the selection of hymns.

"I know one we should sing," exclaimed Martha. "The 'often' hymn."

"The which?" said Gary.

"The 'often' hymn."

He screwed up his face in a characteristic way, mentally ticking off the tune names he knew which began with 'o'.

He shook his head. "I've never heard of it, Martha."

"Oh, yes you have, you've heard it. I know you've heard it. We sing it at school all the time. You know, it goes: 'Oft in danger, oft in woe . . .' "

And so the opening hymn for the burial service was chosen on a note of hope and courage. ('Let not sorrow dim your eye, soon will every tear be dry.') Also, Martha Keys was commissioned to write a special eulogistic sort of poem, and Tricia asked her mother to help find some comforting words for birds in the Scriptures. Mary Felton took time from her busy secretarial job to type the order of service, which follows:

THE FUNERAL OF BA-BA AND HAUKER
Friday, 23 May 1975
4:30 after tea

Opening Hymn:	'Oft in danger, oft in woe Onward, Christian, onward go'
Reading:	Psalm 84
Song:	'I'm not alone for my Father is with me'
Reading:	Matthew 6:25–33
Burial Song:	'Seek Ye First'
Reading:	Poem
Closing Hymn:	'God is working his purpose out'

Burial will be at Yeldall Manor
in the Garden

Even casual observers like Ed Baggett, who was within earshot of the garden, were convinced that what was happening, though couched in child's play, was a true manifestation of the Lord's loving, giving life. We heard the Psalmist's message: that the sparrow had found a house, 'even thine altars, O Lord of Hosts!' And the children's voices piped in heartily as we sang 'Seek ye first the kingdom.' The most troublesome part for the stumbling intellect was when we heard (from Matthew's Gospel), "Why are you anxious for food? Look at the birds, they do not sow or reap or gather into barns, yet your heavenly Father feeds them." One was tempted to wonder why our heavenly father had ignored the hunger of these unfortunate ones.

But as I was pondering this I remembered how the passage had opened: "I am telling you not to worry about your life and what you are to eat . . . Surely life means more than food." And Psalm 84 added the reminder that "A single day in your courts is worth more than a thousand elsewhere."

Now I was beginning to see, to appreciate the significance of these young hearts fervently poured out to nurture, even so briefly, some of the least of God's creatures. *How many tiny birds, I wondered, have ever been so loved, so utterly cared for? After all, they could have died unrescued, without experiencing the gracious, personal touch of the sons of the God who notes every sparrow's fall.*

Now I was recalling our recent community funerals — Yvonne's in January and Andrew's in March. Yvonne had gone to be with the Lord after a long illness, Andrew after a brief infant's lifespan; both had been loved and cared for in our community home. One could see the children acting out in their terms what had first been presented to them in ours. The present experience seemed to reflect what they had absorbed these past months about the reality of death and the meaning of life.

The shoebox containing Ba-Ba and Hauker had now been laid to rest in the grave dug by Johnny, one of the older boys. Jason, aged five, stood by with a bunch of flowers grasped tightly in his right hand. Peering into the open grave, he raised his arm slowly until the bouquet was directly over the hole, then, as if by sudden inspiration, let go. The flowers plummeted to the earth and out of sight into the grave as we all gazed on.

"No, silly," whispered one of the children. "They go on top, after the dirt's put in."

111

Jason looked up innocently, then, standing corrected and obviously eager to please, scrambled to his knees and rescued the soiled flowers. Able-bodied Carl shovelled in the dirt, tamping it down with the toe of his tennis shoe.

What they lack in finesse, I thought, *they surely make up in fervour.*

The strains of the final hymn floated out on the Berkshire breezes, full of hope:

> *God is working his purpose out,*
> *as year succeeds to year . . .*

Yes, surely he is.

I looked around me at the beautiful place the Lord had given us as home: a place to lay our young, to raise them up strong in an awareness of him. And I looked at these young sons who were already manifesting his loving presence to a groaning creation.

We walked back to the house with the closing strains sounding in our ears:

> *Nearer and nearer draws the time,*
> *The time that shall surely be,*
> *When the earth shall be filled with the glory of God*
> *As the waters cover the sea.*

18

A Steeple Chase

"This way, please. Mr. Prickett will see you now."

We were ushered into a small but rather plush London office where a friendly smile and handshake awaited us in the form of Ray Prickett, a recording engineer with Pye Records. He was a thoughtful man, quiet and unassuming. We felt an immediate confidence in him. He listened to a few selections from an album we had made in America and said, "The best thing will be for you to find a church in which to record."

A church, yes, it did seem right somehow since our music was entirely worship-orientated. Besides, it would help keep down recording costs, there was no doubt. We arranged recording dates with Mr. Prickett, to fit into the complex Fisherfolk ministry schedule, and came away satisfied that we were moving in the right direction.

Our steeple chase began with trips to several churches in the south of England. One, reported to have fine acoustics, turned out to be about the size of a shoebox (hardly big enough to accommodate twenty singers plus an entourage of guitarists, percussionists, etc). Still another, a famous abbey, had a beautiful grand piano and lots of room resonance. While Mimi and I stood enjoying its acoustical properties, the deafening roar of a jet plane assaulted the silence. As that faded, another sound crescendoed out of the distance: a heavy lorry gearing down to round the curve outside the abbey. We looked at each other and smiled. Obviously there were many things to consider in selecting a church. The proximity of a military airport (we had passed it on our way but failed to recognise its significance) and the situation of the church near a main road were both spoiling factors.

Our next exploration led us to an Anglican vicarage in the Thames Valley. Answering our knock was an elderly clergyman whose eyes, veritable slits in his narrow forehead, gazed at us down the length of an enormous nose.

"Oh yes," he intoned drearily, "you're one of those. We've had several this morning already."

Not being sure just what we were one of, I hastened to explain our reason for coming. At some point the ice began to crack a bit, and soon Mimi and I were being invited to come inside. We had been mistaken for American tourists in search of ancestral tombstones, but once our mission was explained the vicar's attitude changed to one of mild curiosity.

"You should really try the Roman Catholic church across the way," he said. "It is reported to have fine acoustics, and has been used for local recitals for *yaarhs*."

We thanked him and pursued his lead, telephoning ahead this time for an appointment. The rectory door was opened by a pleasant (if rather protective) housekeeper who informed us that the priest could see us only briefly because he had a service. The priest himself was cordial.

As we talked, he responded with pale-faced alarm to the suggestion that guitars, amplifiers, electrical cords and such like be brought into the holy environs of the church.

"The people of St. ——'s would not tolerate having the church converted into a music hall," he said flatly. There seemed little point in pursuing the matter with him, but then he said, still very soberly, "However, I can put it to them in our church council meeting on Monday next. Not that they will decide, you understand. I make the final decision."

We understood. "Can we have a quick look around the church before we leave? We were told you have a service soon."

"Yes, there's a funeral at two." He motioned with his head for us to follow him, and unlocked the door leading through the sacristy.

Strolling about inside the church, we snapped our fingers; the acoustics seemed good. Gary bounded up the stairs to try the organ in the gallery. I followed. Mimi was walking down the centre aisle below, humming something. *Is that a plainsong melody?* I glanced around and noticed that the priest had entered quietly and was preparing himself for the service. *Or is it something else?* It was a haunting tune hanging in the air in a special sort of way. My thoughts turned back to the organ, where Gary was improvising. When I looked down again the priest was talking to Mimi. In a few minutes she came upstairs.

"He wants to know if we know any music suitable for funerals." Her dark eyes danced.

"Did you tell him we did?"

"Yep."

We grinned at each other, then got right down to the

business of selecting the hymns for the funeral, choosing ones we knew from memory of course! At the conclusion of the service, just before the dismissal, the priest introduced us, thanking us in the presence of the congregation for providing such 'lovely and inspiring' music for them.

"Now, what do you make of that?" I asked Mimi and Gary as we drove home. "That has to be one of the quickest about-faces I have seen in a long time! An hour ago we were complete strangers with a frightening request, and twenty minutes later we were singing at one of his services. Isn't the Lord amazing?"

"The Lord," said Mimi, "is the LORD!" in her particular triumphal way.

"Do you suppose that's the church for the recording?" Gary asked.

"Sure looks like it to me, if the idea is not too distasteful to the church council."

"And Ray okays the acoustics."

"Yes."

A phone call on Tuesday morning gave us one answer. "My decision," the priest said quite formally, "is . . . in the . . . affirmative."

Well done! We rang Ray, who agreed to meet us at the church the following day. This time eight of the Fisherfolk came. Ray's estate car was parked in front of the church as we drove up. He had arrived early and was sitting in one of the back pews. Nodding a greeting to us as we entered, he said pleasantly. "I've just been sitting here listening to the birds."

The birds! We stopped in our tracks.

Sure enough, there was a gleeful chorus of them overhead.

"And the car noises," he continued, matter-of-factly.

The church, located just blocks away from the downtown shopping district, was within earshot of the steady hum of traffic, punctuated by occasional horn toots and squealing brakes.

I don't recall hearing all this the day we were here. How could we have missed it? Then I remembered our interview with the priest and our unexpected singing for the funeral. That was how.

We stood outside around Ray's car feeling a bit deflated. Everything had seemed to point towards this place.

"Perhaps you need to look further afield," he suggested.

"How much longer can you reserve the recording dates for us?" I knew the time was short.

"I will need to know by Monday." This was Wednesday.

"Well, I'm sure the Lord will show us the place," I heard myself saying. "We'll be in touch."

*   *   *

Don't ask me why I'm sure. I'm just sure, that's all. The Lord would not have led us this way in vain. Why just look at the way he has used each encounter. I wonder where he is going to lead us next. It's intriguing, that's what it is, like a half-worked puzzle!

Diane provided the next puzzle-piece as we drove home. "Hey, you guys, you remember that service we did at St. John's College, Oxford? That's a really neat chapel. I like the acoustics."

There were approving sounds.

"But how would you ever use such a place for recording? I mean, they have daily services, don't they?"

"It's open to the public daily, I know for sure."

"I've got it! We could ring Graham Dow, the chaplain. He was so friendly and helpful to us when we were there. Perhaps he could make enquiries for us."

And so we did. And so he did. Fortunately for us the dates we had in mind fell in the middle of the summer break. That seemed quite a favourable factor. Graham promised to have a chat with one of the college officials and meet us in the chapel on Friday.

Driving up the wide expanse of St. Giles Street in the buzzing centre of Oxfordian academia, one could see the college tower less than fifty feet away. How could a building so close to the busy street possibly be quiet enough? Yet when we strolled past the outer wall into the courtyard, the noise ceased, and once inside the lovely sixteenth-century chapel we were in another world, rich with the warmth of wood carvings and coloured by stained glass, quiet and beautiful.

We turned our minds to practical matters. The organ was a fine instrument as we had expected and there was good room resonance.

"What about a piano?" I asked Graham.

"There's not one here. I really don't know . . ."

Knowing that our piano at home was no good for recording (even if we could find a way to transport it) I pursued the matter with him.

"Is there a local music shop where one can hire an instrument for a few days?"

"Oh, I'm sure there must be. Now hang on a minute. I'm just remembering some problem about that." He was silent for a moment. "Now I remember. A friend of mine was in a group, a very outstanding group actually, that needed a piano for a week-long appearance here. They were told that pianos are only hired on a yearly basis."

"Oh, that's not too encouraging, is it?"

"Well no, not really. I wish I could be more helpful."

Graham left us to keep another appointment and we agreed to meet back at the chapel in the early afternoon. Strolling past shop windows after lunch we noticed a music company.

"Well?" Mimi and Gary and I exchanged glances.

"Let's!" said Mimi. "Who knows? They might even say, 'yes'. After all, the Lord knows we need a piano to make this recording. Right?"

"Right!"

So in we went. And out we came half an hour later with a signed agreement for the hiring of an upright piano. Whooppee!

"What about Ray? And what about final approval from the college officials?" Gary asked as we scurried back to the college so as not to keep Graham waiting.

"Ray will be able to drive over sometime this weekend. And Graham's first conversation with the officials was not DIS-couraging. That's the next best thing to EN-couraging. I think we need to forge ahead. After all, we already have a piano!" I waved the receipt in my hand.

Back in the chapel, we sat and soaked in the quiet beauty of the place. Suddenly, from across the chancel, Mimi spoke. "The clock," she said simply.

In the stillness, with all conversations ceasing, one could hear it plainly. "Cuhlock . . . cuhlock . . . cuhlock . . ." The sound was round and substantial, both in timbre and duration.

Graham entered apologising for keeping us waiting.

After telling him the good news about the piano, I said, "There is one thing that worries us a bit: it's the clock in the tower. Even a small sound like that can hinder recording. Do you suppose they could turn it off for us?"

The colour seemed to drain from his face.

"Turn off the clock?" he echoed, looking as if he had seen a ghost. "You must realise . . ." I hated to see him so pained and regretted putting him in such an embarrassing spot. "You must realise one . . . just doesn't . . . TURN OFF THE CLOCK AT OXFORD UNIVERSITY!" he spluttered.

"Yes, I understand it's an unusual request. But the Lord has done such good things so far, and . . ."

"He has even found a piano for us!" Gary chimed in.

"Yes. Well, all right." He stared at us thoughtfully. 'I'll ask." A faint smile relaxed the corners of his mouth. "And you pray."

Monday I waited for Graham to ring me. He was to have talked to the college official first thing that morning. Today was also our last chance to book Ray's recording time.

At eleven o'clock, a voice came over the intercom, "Mr. Prickett on line 3 for you."

"All right." *It's not all right at all. What am I going to tell him?*

"Hello . . . Ray? . . . you did drive over? . . . everything seems good about the building. Yes, that's what we thought too . . . Who did you say? . . ." *Another group is pressurising him about the recording dates we wanted so he needs an answer.* "Yes, well . . . I had hoped . . ."

Mary was a little breathless as she handed me the phone message. "It's Graham Dow on the other line."

"Ray? Can you hang on a minute?"

"I took the message," Mary continued, "because I knew

120

you were on the phone to Mr. Prickett. Graham Dow says all systems are go for recording at St. John's. The University officials are willing to stop the clock for you. He seemed excited."

"I'm excited too! O praise the Lord. Are you still there, Ray? Yes, well the answer is YES. Those dates will be fine. Everything has been approved, even the stopping of the clock. Isn't that great?"

Super timing, Lord. Really super. Couldn't have been better, I mean closer. A real photofinish.

... Now let's see ... It seems to me there was a time when you caused the sun to stand still. That was really something. Lord, for you stopping clocks must seem a small thing really. But it's a big thing to us. Thank you.

* The album *Songs from Sound of Living Waters* was recorded in the chapel of St. John's College, Oxford University in July 1974.

121

19

A Tale of Two Trousers.

"Mama, why are we so poor?" Seven-year-old David's up-turned face was trusting, his voice gentle with entreaty.

"Well," I paused and gazed out of the window towards the sea, "I think it's so that God can show us how rich he is. You see, David, when you are rich, it's very hard to know that what you have comes from God. It's easy to think you earned it or deserved it somehow."

"Jim is poorer than we are."

"You mean Jim your classmate?"

"Yes, no one cares for him properly. I feel sorry for him."

"I understand. Because not being cared for is the worst kind of being poor there is, isn't it?"

He nodded.

"Do you think God cares for you?"

Another affirmative nod.

"Would you like to hear a story about how God cared for someone we know? Well then, come hop on my lap. Here it is.

"Once upon a time there was a tall, lanky, blond boy named Bill, who was 15 years old."

"My brother Bill?" he asked excitedly.

"Yes, your brother Bill. Like most 15-year-old boys, he was growing v-e-r-y fast. Do you know that, in one year, he grew a foot?"

David thrust his right foot out for inspection.

"Not that kind of foot, silly. He grew twelve inches — that's as long as a whole ruler! We kept a measurement on the kitchen door. That's how I remember.

"Now back in those days the Lord had begun to teach us a few things about living more simply. Do you know what a charge account is?"

David shook his head from side to side.

"Well, it's an agreement you make with a store so that you can buy things now and pay for them later."

"Oh, that's very nice of them."

"Yes, very. So if we were in a store and you saw a toy you liked, but we had no cash on hand, we could just say, 'Charge it, please,' and take it home with us straight away."

"Oh, lovely!"

"Guess what, David."

"What?"

"Sometimes it's not so lovely."

"Why not?"

"Just suppose that we charged that toy to our account — let's say it cost five pounds. And next month you wanted very much to buy a gift for your cousin Colleen who had been in hospital. Also your wellingtons had come apart and your feet were getting very cold and wet so you needed new boots, but instead of getting those things you would have to pay for the toy you had charged last month and . . ."

"I know!" David snapped his fingers with alacrity. "We could just go to another shop and say 'Charge it please,' like we did before."

"Yes. Well, I'm afraid that's exactly what a lot of people do. And do you know what? It gets them into a heap of trouble eventually. It's a lot simpler to spend what you have than to spend what you don't have yet. So that's what the Lord encouraged us to do back then, when Bill was a teenager.

"Now Bill had a wonderful pair of blue, black and white checked trousers. They were ever so handsome, his favourite pair. In fact they were his only really nice ones. I noticed how they were getting shorter and shorter and tighter and tighter, and one morning Bill appeared at the breakfast table looking very dejected, with the blue trousers in his hand.

" 'I just can't get into my trousers anymore,' he said.

" 'Oh dear. And they're your best ones, aren't they?' I replied. 'Well, never mind, I'm sure the Lord will send along some new ones.'

"Now mind you, we didn't have any charge accounts, so I couldn't just hop down to the shop and buy him some new ones. Not only that, our cash on hand was very limited at that time of month, so we might have to wait several weeks just to consider this need along with many other needs in the household.

"Bill's face brightened all of a sudden and he said, 'Hey, Mom! I know what. I bet these would just fit Billy.' Billy was a friend of Bill's whose father was a full-time worker at the church, in charge of maintenance. So Bill took his beloved blue checked trousers and gave them to his friend Billy. He looked much happier after he had thought of this, and I was glad."

"Did he get some more trousers?"

"Not yet.

"Now that very morning, while Bill was away at school, I was cleaning the house and taking care of you."

"Was I a baby?"

"Yes, you were about eight months old then, and your hair stuck straight up on top of your head."

"Did I look funny?"

"Oh, a bit. You were a very happy baby; you loved to sit and listen to music and sway back and forth in your playpen."

David giggled.

"While I was looking after you that morning, a friend of mine named Wanda came by for a visit. She lived thirty miles from Houston in a small town, but she loved to come in for special meetings at the church, and sometimes just to see us. This particular morning we had a good chat, and she was telling me about the comings and goings of her large family. She has nine children."

"That's more than us!"

"Yes. Before she left, she pointed to a box she had brought in and said, 'Here are some odds and ends, a few outgrown shirts of Tuffy's and I forget what else. I thought some of the children might be able to use them.'

"I'm sure they can, I said, and after she had gone, I took a quick look in the box, just to get an idea what was there."

"Oh, I hope there were some trousers for Bill!" David's

125

lithe body was fairly dancing on my lap. The combination of an active imagination and a genuine love for his brother had his motor racing.

"Well, as a matter of fact, there were some trousers. Can you guess what kind?"

"Some that were exactly right for Bill," he piped.

"You can say that again. Why, do you know when I lifted out the shirts in the top of the box, there, underneath them lay a pair of blue and black and white checked trousers, just like the ones Bill had given away!"

'You mean, the very same?"

"That's what I mean. Even the manufacturer's tag was the same."

David clapped his hands together.

'There was one small difference, however," I continued. "These trousers were a size larger than the ones he had given away, so that meant they would fit Bill perfectly."

"Oh, I knew it, I knew it!" David chirped with glee.

"I laid them out on his bed so he would find them when he came home from school. Do you think he was surprised?"

David nodded. "Very," he said. "And happy too."

"Do you know, David, that when we give to others and trust the Lord to take care of us, he always does?"

"Yes," came a soft reply, as I tucked him in bed.

"You know what, Mother?"

"What?"

"I love God very much."

"I know you do." A kiss on the cheek. "Good night, David."

"Good night."

20

Wee Georgie

I picked up his cage because he seemed so strangely still. Thoughts flooded my mind: *I should have taken the cage downstairs last night. I remember thinking, 'This is going to be our coldest night.' Oh . . . why didn't I?* Martha was pulling on her robe and finding her slippers, shivering slightly from the chill December morning in her unheated room. *I always was worried about the little creature surviving the cold Scottish winter,* my thoughts continued. *Oh, if only I had taken him downstairs to the one warm room. But then, of course, there were the cats to worry about.*

"Martha," I said, "I'm afraid . . . little George . . . got too cold last night." His body was stiff in the corner of the cage.

"Oh, George!" The tremulous voice well suited the fervency of her ten-year-old loving heart.

Then there was a moment of quiet.

"Oh Mommie, let's take him down where it's warm."

There was a fire in the fireplace of our downstairs bedroom. We placed the cage on the hearth, and by now

Martha's tears were streaming freely down her face. She opened the cage and lifted out his stiff body.

"He's just asleep. We need to get some brandy for him ... you know, like Aunt Gerry gave him the time he was sick at Yeldall. And we'll keep him here by the fire where it's warm." Her words tumbled out.

"But honey, I really think . . ."

"Mother, please go find the brandy."

From across the room we heard Graham's voice. "Is there a soft cloth to lay him on?"

I looked, and meanwhile in the background we could hear Martha's softly sobbing voice as she knelt by the hearth. "Oh Lord Jesus . . . please . . . give him life."

A few moments passed, and then Martha's voice, a little stronger now, "Look! His ear moved!"

I trained my gaze upon the shrunken form of this miserable little rodent — marvelling somehow at the love Martha obviously had for him. I saw nothing. Or did I? I knelt at the hearth, and while I held the cloth containing Georgie, Martha ran to find the brandy.

Oh Jesus, I've never prayed for a rat. Oh Lord, for Martha . . . who loves him so . . . Lord, hear her prayer.

In a few minutes the door opened and I saw Cathleen's ample form. In her left arm she held baby Virginia Clare, and in her right a small container of brandy and an eyedropper. Martha followed closely on her heels. As Cathleen gently administered the last rites of brandy to the little gerbil, she said softly, very matter-of-factly, "You know, Martha, sometimes gerbils do grow old and die, and sometimes that's the best thing for them."

The thought registered and Martha said simply, "But George isn't old."

There was another slight jerk in one of George's ears. I looked at the clock. "Oh! We barely have time to get dressed for the service."

"Just leave George here by the hearth where it's warm, and let's see what the Lord will do." Graham's voice was calm and clear. He had not been well, and consequently would not be attending the morning service; so he could keep an eye on George.

A special surprise awaited the congregation on this first Sunday in Advent. No organ prelude would greet them but rather, out of the silence, a crisp, clear sound, "Awake, o sleeper, rise up from the dead, and Christ will give you light!" The choir was singing a round, written by one of the Fisherfolk just a year ago, and in its own buoyant, staccato style it conveyed the same message as the magnificent 'Wachet auf'* which Christians would be singing the world over on this Sunday: awake, arise, trim your lamps, go forth to meet the bridegroom! What expectancy . . . and hope . . . and joy. In the sermon we heard how God has chosen to reveal himself most powerfully through that which is weak, ill-esteemed, despised by men. "Behold, your king is coming to you, humble, and mounted on an ass, and on a colt, the foal of an ass."

The service ended, Martha made a bee-line for our room and I followed. A peaceful fireside scene greeted us. Graham was out of bed now, wrapped in a warm robe, sitting by the fire reading. Beside him on the hearth stood the gerbil cage. Did our eyes deceive us, or was that really George we saw running about the cage, climbing the bars, and frisking here and there?

"Oh — Georgie!" Martha's delight knew no bounds.

*Sleepers, wake.

"Mother, you remember, in church, you remember? We sang that song about awake, o sleeper, rise up from the dead . . . well, George heard it!"

Graham chuckled in a warm, fatherly sort of way. "Yep, I guess he did. He surely is alive and kicking now."

We stood and simply watched him for a few minutes as he skittered about his cage. We stood in awe of the God who uses warmth and brandy, and the prayers of one of his little saints to restore and quicken, bringing life out of death.

"Say, Martha," her daddy said, "I can't see any food or water in this cage, and George seems to be chewing the metal bars."

"Oh, I know. I need to fill his water jar. And Tricia has some sunflower seeds she'll let me have. I'll run and get them."

"Good," said Graham. He looked at the gerbil with an understanding smile.

" 'After all,' says George, 'what's the use of being alive if there's nothing to eat or drink.'!"

21

Gale Warning

"Are the boats running?"

"You think he'll get across all right?"

The wind from the southwest was picking up velocity, and that meant rough seas and treacherous landings at the ferry slip on Cumbrae Island. Ray Prickett was on his way from London to do three days of recording with us.

"Sure. He'll make it."

At our last session with him at St. John's College chapel in Oxford, I remembered telling Ray about our imminent move to Scotland. "Is there any possibility you could come that far to record for us?" I had asked. "The small cathedral there is reported to have fine acoustics."

"And no airplane noise to interfere, I would imagine," he added with a twinkle in his eye, recalling our earlier search for a good recording location in the south of England. A friend at Heathrow Airport had even helped us study the air traffic patterns!

"No indeed. It's a small island off the west coast. Oh incidentally, it's approachable only by ferry."

'Well, if the ferry will accommodate my estate car, I'm

ready to come," Ray had said with one of his boyish grins.

And here he was. In February's late-afternoon darkness we unloaded his precious cargo of recording equipment. I marvelled at his adaptability. The former sacristy, now turned communications office, was once again being transformed — this time into a control room by Ray. His skilful eye scanned the room and within minutes the desks and tables were rearranged to studio specifications. After dinner several of the Fisherfolk helped him set up mikes in the cathedral.

"We're all set for tomorrow," they reported around nine o'clock.

*　　*　　*

At half past eight the next morning our valiant troupe of singers, ten strong, turned up for the first recording session. Their costumes betrayed the icy state of the cathedral, unheated except for a few butane tanks which were rolled in for the occasion. Blankets, hot water bottles, three socks per foot, wool scarves and mittens were the order of the day. What an entourage! Our breath control exercises made a splendid show as ten puffs of hot air burst in unison upon the bone-chilling dampness of the cathedral.

After 'warming up' (if one dared call it that) we took a short break to thaw a bit before beginning the recording in earnest. Virginia burst into the warm sitting-room, her plastic coat and boots glistening wet. "The boats are off," she said excitedly. "I've just come back from the ferry slip." A social worker, she and the teenage school children were our only regular commuters to the mainland.

"Force eight gales are expected for the next three days according to the weather station at Prestwick," she called back over her shoulder, slightly breathless as she headed for the phone. "I've got to ring the office so they'll know I'm marooned." She paused, her eyes widening. "What about the recording? How can you manage?"

"Oh, we'll manage," came a cheery answer from one of the Fisherfolk. I glanced outside where young Colleen O'Meara was being helped on her way to school by two of the older children. More accurately, she was being anchored to the ground by them, being a tiny lass and prone to blow away in the wrong direction!

My glance travelled to the top of the cathedral spire. Beautifully situated, erect and tall and majestic near the southern tip of the island, the tiny neo-Gothic cathedral seemed to both welcome and challenge the wind and sea. Glancing down the high-pitched rooftop to the lawn beneath, I noticed several slates which had fallen to the ground during the night. In the midst of winter storms, the slate shingles would rattle and make quite a clatter inside the building. The surrounding ridge of hills to the northwest formed a natural wind-tunnel and set up a powerful roaring as the wind swept past the cathedral. During such gales, one could understand how the original spire of the cathedral had been toppled while the scaffolding still stood around it. Now that we had rid ourselves of noisy nuisances like airplanes and motorcars, and had fled industrialisation, we had only God's own noises to contend with. Clearly the matter was beyond our control and in his.

"Well, if the worst comes to the worst, you can all sleep during the day and sing at night!" Virginia was back now.

"Providing the weather calms down then," she added hopefully.

"Whatever is needed to make these three days of recording count for us, that's what we're ready to do," I answered. "After all, we asked the Lord to stop us if these were not his chosen days. We asked him that months ago, and we asked him especially to control the weather for us, and . . ."

"And besides all that, he has done great and impossible things before," Ed chimed in.

"You'd better believe he has. Do you remember the Villa?"

There was a warmth of recognition in many faces and 'hmms' of assent.

"No, I don't remember the Villa at all," said Richard, one of the newer Fisherfolk. He was from Scotland.

"Well, no wonder. That was B.B."

"It was what?"

"Before Britain." Max laughed.

"Well, you see," Pat Allen went on to explain in her peace-filled way, "we had never done a recording in a church before, everything was new to us. We were accustomed to standing close to each other in the Redeemer choir stalls and having our organist just a few feet away. When we had an opportunity to record a eucharist live in the chapel of the Villa de Matel, a Roman Catholic convent, we were unprepared for lots of things that were different, to say the least."

"Like standing two feet apart in the choir stalls!" Conway chuckled. "We couldn't hear each other at all. We really felt lost."

"And sounded the same," I added with a smile. "After

all, we were not exactly the Roger Wagner Chorale! We had strong singers and weak singers, and the weak relied on the strong . . ."

"And what about poor George away up in the balcony?" We laughed, remembering how far away our faithful friend and organist had seemed.

"We couldn't hear him, and he couldn't see us!"

"And the organ was badly out of tune."

"Do you know," I was remembering soberly, "that within twenty-four hours everything that had been topsy-turvy was set right, the organ got a last-minute tuning, the Lord showed us a different place to stand so we could hear . . ."

"And George played every note from memory, watching you in the mirror," Mimi added.

"Yes, I well remember. He never took his eyes off me."

There was a long pause.

"It was an unforgettable experience," Pat said in her soft, deep way. "The Lord was there."

"Yes."

"And he's here today, too," she added gently, smiling at me.

"Let's go and sing."

And sing we did throughout the day, gales notwithstanding. Somehow the strong southwesterly winds blowing up from the sea seemed diverted from the cathedral itself.

The second morning offered a greater challenge. Strolling through the sound room at half past eight I could hear distinctly the moaning of the wind through Ray's tape recorder.

"The wind's blowing up quite a bit this morning," he

remarked with equanimity. That's what I appreciated about Ray: he was always cool as a cucumber when the fiery trials came. Several of the Fisherfolk passed through on their way to tune instruments. There was a certain sobriety about our preparations that day. I marvelled at the calm, quiet way the team went about their business, without distraction or fluster. Despite the din of noise coming against the building outside, they were confidently tuning up for the recording the Lord had promised us.

Force eight gale or better! my thoughts said. Walking through the nave, I noticed the west window and was reminded of its history. During the building of the cathedral all of the workmen escaped injury and as a thank offering to God for his mercies donated the beautiful window. Later on, the story goes, during a severe storm the entire window shattered and blew in upon a worshipping congregation. Again, quite miraculously, no one was hurt.

The Lord has been performing miracles in this place for a long time, I reminded myself. As we gathered in the choir stalls to pray, my thoughts flashed back to a windy campsite in Kentucky where, years ago, we had pitched our tents during a family holiday trip. A violent midsummer storm blew up, the wind beat against the tent wall and the pegs beneath the tent began to strain in the rain-soaked earth. I was frightened. Then I noticed that, wonder of wonders, everyone else in the tent was asleep. In the next instant the Lord reminded me how he had spoken to the wind once, as a master would to his barking dog, or a parent to his whimpering child. And so I had said quite simply, *Peace be still.* And in a few moments the wind ceased its beating upon the tent and the ropes stopped their straining, and a wonderful quiet settled over the tent. I thanked the Lord and went to sleep.

Mike was praying for us now, "Lord, the wind is yours, and we are yours. We offer you this recording time and ask you to glorify yourself in it."

We took our places for recording.

"We're ready," I said over the mike to Ray in the next room.

"Just hang on a minute. There's a bit of wind noise coming over."

We waited — possibly twenty seconds.

"It's fading now. We're all set, rolling."

The red light flashed and we began to sing. All morning we sang. Only once did Ray stop us. He came out of his hideaway and said, "There was a chorus of birds outside at the end of that last number."

"Oh? Shall we do it again then?"

He smiled.

"No, I don't think so." His eyes twinkled merrily, "I rather liked it actually."

The tune was one of Mimi's and the birds must have come to add their melodic benediction to the words: "Trust in the Lord with all thine heart; lean not unto thine own understanding. In all thy ways acknowledge him, and he shall direct thy paths."

Yes Lord, it's true.

* The album *Songs from Fresh Sounds* was among the recordings made in the Cathedral of the Isles, Cumbrae, Scotland, during February 1976. During three days of recording during heavy winter gales, less than ten minutes of recording time was lost on account of wind noise.

22

A College goes to Heaven

It was an unusual Sunday . . . February 29, 1976. 'God's merciful care of us' was the theme of our Sunday afternoon family church meeting. It had just ended and we were filing out as the cathedral chimes rang four.

"There's a fire! In the North College!" Jodi's lips were drawn, her face white as she slipped past me in the cloister.

"Check this building. All the children should be taken to the Annexe."

A bucket brigade was forming, twelve strong, from the outside washroom of the South College, as we waited for the fire engine to come. The fire appeared to have started in the bedroom at the southern tip of the college. It should be easy to control.

After a minute with the water taps on full blast, the first bucket was only a quarter full.

"There's no water pressure."

"There's got to be."

"There isn't."

Our senses strained for some sign of the fire engine's approach.

The children filed obediently into the Annexe, a safe fifty feet away from the North College. Cars were moved to make plenty of space for the local volunteer fire department.

After minutes which seemed like hours they arrived and sprang into action. The nearest hydrant was 200 yards away at the end of the narrow driveway which led down to the street. The volunteers were quick on their feet and confident of controlling the flames. But alas! The task was impossible. Our hearts sank. After several minutes of determined effort, one of the volunteers called out, "Send for the mainland brigade!"

The nearest town on the mainland was a fifteen-minute ferry ride away plus ten extra minutes by land. The wind seemed to be picking up, blowing hard from the southwest. At least it was blowing in the opposite direction from the other buildings in the cathedral complex. For that we could be thankful, since the closest structure was a mere ten feet away.

But the grim truth soon came hard upon us: our fire-fighting equipment was woefully inadequate and the wind was driving the fire rapidly northward through the rectangular length of the building. So far the fire was contained on the first floor, and at this point an evacuation of furnishings and office equipment from the ground floor beneath was undertaken. Many of the villagers had gathered to be of help. Within twenty minutes the interior of the cathedral was scarcely recognisable as stacks of furnishings, personal belongings, books and typewriters were hastily deposited on the tile floor. People worked quietly, quickly. There was an incredible pain and a remarkable peace present.

"It's gonna' go."

"Everyone out of the building."

All the carrying out and passing from hand to hand ceased. We stood and looked at the home where twenty-three of us lived. The children were brought quietly from the Annexe around to the front of the college, each child with an adult, because it seemed good that they should see with their own eyes what they already sensed in their hearts to be a momentous event. We comforted them.

"Will my toys be all right?" enquired four-year-old Will Kennedy as Virginia carried him past the cathedral.

"I'm afraid they may not be able to save them, Will," she answered him. He began to cry.

"But," Virginia continued, "the Lord can always provide more toys, you know." He became quiet.

Then he lifted his head from her shoulder and said cheerily, "Yeah! ... and we can always make paper airplanes!" He dried his dark almond-shaped eyes on his shirtsleeve.

We stood still and watched the bulging, melting rooftop give way and the flames leap skyward. More smoke billowed from windows. The wind fanned the flames northward at an ever-increasing tempo. The entire first floor had become an inferno.

The silence was strong. The sense of loss was great. The shock was deep.

Bill Farra stood on the lawn in his dressing-gown and slippers. He had been ill and resting in his room when the fire began. That explained why he had been on hand to rescue twenty-month-old Jeremiah from his cot. Only later did we hear the whole story: how his first attempt failed because of the heavy smoke in the hallway, and how it happened that he fled downstairs and re-entered the building, mounting the central staircase close to Jeremiah's bedroom.

Now he stood outside on the chilly damp ground shivering occasionally from the wind gusts. His room at the north end of the building was burning brightly. As we watched, through the crowd burst fifteen-year-old Carter bringing his own new pair of blue jeans to Bill. His face was a study in shock and sorrow, in great earnestness and concern. It was the first of many such gestures we were to see over the coming days, as people both within and without our community and indeed, friends from all over the world sent us help. But first the help came in particular ways like this: from our children, from neighbours in Millport who opened their homes to us, and through encouraging dreams like David's.

David was seven, and was especially concerned for Max who (like most of the Fisherfolk) had lost all of his clothing in the fire. He was particularly sad about Max's fine new cowboy shirt and fancy suede boots, a gift from his parents whom he had recently visited in Texas.

The day after the fire, David came to us with his blue eyes dancing. "I had a dream," he said. "I dreamt that the North College died and went to heaven. And when Jesus saw Max's cowboy shirt he put it on straight away and said, 'My, that's a fine shirt! I'll be proud to wear it.' And when he saw his new pair of suede boots, he put them on and said, 'Now, I've been needing a pair of warm boots, and look! They fit me perfectly!' "

Amidst the pain of loss, of separation from the familiar (whether a favourite photograph, a treasured letter or a pair of old slippers) the Lord was showing us the eternal freshness, the new-every-morning-ness of his life springing up in unquenchable ways. Especially we were seeing it in the children's responses.

Digging around the charred ruins of the North College, ten-year-old Martha came across the slightly toasted frontispiece to a book. She brought it to me triumphantly, with the air of someone who had found an important something. It read, 'Everything was beautiful, and nothing was hurt.'

In the quiet acceptance of loss lay the beauty, against a charred and tragic backdrop; I could see it, touch it, feel it as my friends suffered the loss of their most treasured 'things'. (They had few at the outset.) In the providence of God and in his marvellous protecting power lay our safekeeping. His care of us, as we had just been saying on that leap-year Sunday, is never wanting. His mercies fail not.

Everything was beautiful.
And nothing was hurt.
Thanks be to God.

a short history of fisherfolk ministries

The first seeds of Fisherfolk ministries were sown over fourteen years ago in Houston, Texas. A significant renewal at the Episcopal Church of the Redeemer led to change in every area of life—worship, fellowship, leadership, outreach ministry, educational programs, and youth and children's ministries. New family life and church vitality became visible, and the excitement began to spread. Groups of young people began travelling extensively in the United States to share the message of renewal, and the rector of the Church of the Redeemer, Rev. Graham Pulkingham, received invitations for speaking engagements from other churches both in America and abroad.

Rev. Pulkingham went to England on such a speaking tour in 1972. That visit resulted in an invitation from the Bishop of Coventry, who had seen a CBS television special on the Houston church, for Mr. Pulkingham and a group from the church to come live and work in the Coventry diocese. They did so in September 1972, settling in a parish in Potter's Green, where they became involved with the church's life, leadership, and ministry.

They were joined in February 1973 by seven others from the Houston church—members of a travelling outreach team. Named the Fisherfolk upon their arrival in Great Britain, these young people continued to travel and spread their message of renewal, but soon were unable to meet the increasing demands for their ministry. In June 1973 seven more members made the move across the Atlantic.

This addition brought the number of people in the community to thirty—too many to fit their accommodation in Coventry. As there was no property available in the Coventry Diocese, the community looked further afield. Through the kindness of the Abbot of Nashdom Abbey, they were offered a disused convent in Berkshire. In October 1973 the community, now known as The Community of Celebration, began the extensive cleaning project necessary to make the lovely manor house and grounds their home.

The move to Yeldall Manor coincided with another expansion. The travelling ministries of Mr. Pulkingham and the Fisherfolk had generated much interest in the community's lifestyle and ministry. Several English churches sent lay leaders and their families to live in the community for a year, to be trained in common life and shared ministry. Other English folk joined the teams, which by then numbered three. By December 1974, the membership of the entire community approached ninety persons.

Again it seemed the community was to outgrow its accommodation. Mr. Pulkingham was invited by the Bishop of Argyll and the Isles to establish a ministry of renewal on the property of the Cathedral of the Isles on the Isle of Cumbrae. Part of the Bishop's concern was the provision of a minister for the Cathedral congregation. To meet this need, Mr. Pulkingham was offered the position of Provost of the Cathedral. He accepted, and in August 1975 about one-third of the Berkshire community moved to Scotland. Of the remaining two-thirds, quite a number, including one entire Fisherfolk team, went to Dorset to live and work at Post Green, a sister community; others returned to the English churches from which they had come for training; a few returned to the U.S.A., where they were joined by others from the Church of the Redeemer in the formation of another Fisherfolk community in Woodland Park, Colorado; and one household remained behind in Berkshire to support the village vicar in his ministry.

Today the Community of Celebration in Scotland is composed of about fifty people representing five nationalities and various denominational backgrounds. They support themselves by income from recordings and books and by owning and running the local bakery. In addition, the Cumbrae family is involved in developing the eleven-acre farm on which the Cathedral of the Isles is located, with an eye to making their lifestyle more self-sufficient. Research and development in areas of Christian nurture, lifestyle, and worship continue, and the fruit of such research is shared throughout the world—Celebration Services, International produces records and tapes, and publishes music and teaching kits which include drama, dance, poetry, music and mime. The Community of Celebration in Scotland is linked by fellowship with other like-minded communities in the U.S.A., England, Australia, and Sweden, and together this community of communities seeks to explore the radical call to discipleship in a rapidly changing world.